When Graduation's Over, Learning Begins

When Graduation's Over, Learning Begins

Lessons for STEM Students and Professionals

Roger Forsgren

BEP

BUSINESS EXPERT PRESS

Leader in applied, concise business books

When Graduation's Over, Learning Begins:
Lessons for STEM Students and Professionals

Cover design by Charlene Kronstedt

About the cover photo: The view of the earth from the International Space Station's cupola window. *Source*: National Aeronautics and Space Administration.

Interior design by Exeter Premedia Services Private Ltd., Chennai, India

First published in 2023 by
Business Expert Press, LLC
222 East 46th Street, New York, NY 10017
www.businessexpertpress.com

ISBN-13: 978-1-63742-436-0 (paperback)
ISBN-13: 978-1-63742-437-7 (e-book)

Business Expert Press Portfolio and Project Management Collection

First edition: 2023

10 9 8 7 6 5 4 3 2 1

To my four grandsons: John, Andy, Myles, and Charlie.

Promise me you'll always remember: you're braver than you believe, and stronger than you seem, and smarter than you think.
—Christopher Robin

Description

What They Didn't Teach You in School: Lessons for STEM Students and Professionals

Science, Technology, Engineering, and Math (STEM) education has been described as *drinking from a firehose*. STEM students are required to absorb an overwhelming amount of technical information before they can earn their undergraduate degrees. But it takes more than a thorough understanding of math, science, and engineering concepts to become successful in today's job market.

NASA's former Chief Knowledge Officer, Roger Forsgren, was responsible for training the agency's technical workforce and, in the following pages, provides *critical lessons learned for STEM* students and graduates to build successful careers as they compete in today's workplace.

- **Being an introvert in an extroverts' world**: You may certainly be *the smartest person in the room*, but that may not be enough to convince a client, make a persuasive presentation, or effectively manage others. Learn how to remain in your comfort zone yet still make a compelling impact by becoming an *ambivert*.
- **Communication skills**: How to get your point across and express yourself in a cogent, concise manner. *How to make yourself heard, and respected*, in a group of experienced professionals.
- **Critical thinking**: Avoid jumping to conclusions by training yourself to *look beyond the obvious* for the real clues to a problem or situation.
- **Ethics**: STEM professionals possess unique skills, but such technical expertise also requires a sense of personal responsibility *ensuring your talents are being put to the best use* for yourself and for society.

Case studies have proven to be valuable learning tools, and Roger Forsgren includes 12 compelling historical case studies that demonstrate the *critical knowledge needed for STEM students* as they progress through their careers.

Keywords

NASA; training; STEM; STEAM; introvert; ambivert; communication skills; critical thinking; engineering ethics; what they didn't teach you; case studies; lessons learned; soft skills; people skills; engineering education; Bob Ebeling; Challenger; Abilene Paradox; Herbert Hoover; Neil Armstrong; Mann Gulch; Wag Dodge; Mars Surveyor; Mars Climate Orbiter ; Mars Polar Lander; Robert E. Lee; Gettysburg; Socratic method; cognitive bias; sudden infant death syndrome; SIDS; thymicolymphaticus; Abraham Wald; Phineas Gage; ethics vs. morals; Dieselgate; Arvind Thiruvengadam; Hemanth Kappanna; Marc Besch; Oliver Schmidt; Apollo 12; SCE to AUX; Is it ever permissible to tell a lie?; Albert Speer; Germania; scorched earth; John Stuart Mill

Contents

Testimonials

"Forsgren's deep knowledge and years of experience shines through. The book boasts a treasure chest of practical guides and actionable strategies to improve effective communication and developing problem-solving skills."—**Minoo Rathnasabapathy, PhD, Research Engineer, MIT Media Lab, Project Fellow, Future of Space, World Economic Forum**

"Roger Forsgren possesses a rare trait for an engineer—amazing storyteller. He clearly has a passion for seeing the engineering profession succeed and uses this book to succinctly address the human and ethical components that are required to be successful in the STEM world. This should be compulsory reading for all engineering students or as part of a Professional Engineering Certification." —**Brock Brown MA, CPHR, Certified S.C.C. Executive Coach**

"Roger Forsgren has successfully created an engaging book that reminds recent STEM graduates that it's not just about the technology, it's also about people. *All of today's STEM graduates should read this book before they walk across the stage at graduation to embark on their careers."*—**Dr. Pierre LaRochelle, Department Head and Professor of Mechanical Engineering, South Dakota School of Mines & Technology**

"This is a must read for engineers and STEM students learning critical skills to great career success. I'm going to offer it as a resource in my course 'The Best Teams: Introverts, Ambiverts and Extroverts' Roger has walked the talk at NASA. Reading this book is like sitting down with a wise elder and getting extremely useful sage advice."—**Bob Faw, Chief Energizing Officer, Matchbox Group**

"This is a compelling collection of case studies and personal profiles ranging from the Mann Gulch Fire to Lee at Gettysburg to Albert Speer that will be useful to engineers just beginning their career as well as seasoned veterans who are moving into managerial positions.

Forsgren's experience as a NASA engineer with a background in the liberal arts has given him the depth and breadth necessary to offer unique perspectives on a well-chosen set of historical events and personalities."—**Dr. Blaine Lilly, Professor Emeritus, College of Engineering, Ohio State University**

Introduction

I graduated from college with a liberal arts degree. I was always fascinated with history but soon discovered there weren't many jobs available for history majors. Desperate for work, I was eventually hired by the National Aeronautics and Space Administration (NASA) as an apprentice mechanic. At the time, it felt like an embarrassing step backward for a college grad to earn a living turning wrenches. I was an historian trying to learn how to run a lathe, weld aluminum, bend tubing, and calibrate torque wrenches.

During my four-year apprenticeship program at NASA, I was rotated among various buildings and shops to learn a variety of skills from the different tradesmen I was assigned to. After each tour of duty, I would meet with the area supervisor who would then give me an appraisal of my work and my progress in becoming a journeyman. During the course of one interview, I mentioned that I had a college degree from Georgetown University where I had studied the liberal arts with a major in history. I thought my background might impress him, but this manager looked directly at me and said, "I'm really sorry to hear that." Taken aback, I asked why, and he responded, "Well, for this job you don't need a college education and I feel bad that you spent so many years and so much money earning a degree only to get a job where you don't need it." This wasn't the last time at NASA, where almost everyone held advanced technical degrees, that my liberal arts background was met with a bewildering look or occasionally, even ridicule.

A few years later, now a journeyman mechanic, I assembled scientific hardware for experiments that flew aboard the Space Shuttle. I enjoyed working with my hands and my fellow technicians, but I wanted more and enrolled in night school to get an engineering degree. After eight long years, I finally succeeded.

At NASA, I had the good fortune to have participated in almost every role on a project team. From the mechanic fabricating and assembling hardware, to the mechanical engineer designing components, to the systems engineer making it all fit and work together, to the deputy project manager organizing schedules, to the project manager making decisions. I had the unique opportunity to see engineering and project management from several different roles and vantage points. Reflecting back after more than 38 years at NASA, an organization almost completely devoted to technical precision and expertise, I realized the genuine benefits of my liberal arts background. My history degree that once seemed a pointless and expensive effort allowed me to view things objectively and permitted me to think differently, to understand there may be a wider and more complex range of issues behind most engineering and management decisions.

I firmly believe liberal arts made me a better engineer and, as my career evolved more from technical engineering and into managing projects and people, I used my liberal arts degree much more than I used my engineering degree. Actually, after spending a good bit of my career feeling somewhat embarrassed having a history degree, I now consider my background in liberal arts to have been a significant blessing.

I discovered that a more diverse background allows an engineer to approach problems from a different standpoint. It provides an ability to look at design with a more broad or comprehensive perspective considering such issues as maintainability, manufacturability, ergonomics, and design aesthetics rather than concentrating primarily on dimensions, material selection, and functionality. It equips one with an ability to explain complicated designs, decisions, or situations more clearly, particularly in written memos and e-mails. Awareness of the liberal arts, and for me a strong background in history, allowed an understanding and appreciation of the human element that is intricately involved in every engineering design. Unlike mechanisms, electronic circuits, and software algorithms that we find so compelling and personally fulfilling, each human is uniquely different, and significantly more complicated than engineering hardware.

Later in my NASA career, I became the head for training and knowledge management. In this role, I convened a meeting at the Astronauts' Beach House at the Kennedy Space Center. The Beach House had been used by all of the flight crews from Mercury, Gemini, Apollo, and then the Space Shuttle program. It was here that the astronauts and their families and friends gathered for one last barbeque before their flight. It was a tradition for each crew to select a bottle of wine to share when they returned from their mission and place it in a wine cabinet.

I invited several prominent engineering educators from some of the world's best schools to discuss how NASA can better train our newly hired engineers. We called it the *Fifth Year Program* because the critical question I asked our team of experts was: "If you had an extra year at your school to train your engineers, what subjects would you cover?"

For three days, we discussed this and then mapped out a new curriculum we would introduce at NASA. All of us agreed that engineers leave school, after four very intense years, well versed in math and science and engineering principles. The unanimous consensus of these educators, if given an additional fifth year of study, would be to focus on teaching their students better communication skills, decision-making skills, and a more thorough understanding of the ethical responsibilities of their profession. Learning these skills would not only make them better engineers, better leaders, better team members but would also make them better people.

This book is a summary of what I learned at the Astronaut Beach House during those hot and muggy summer days, as well as what I learned after more than 38 years of working among NASA's talented and accomplished technical workforce. In a nutshell, this book focuses on everything they didn't teach you as you earned your STEM degree. Or, perhaps better: everything they didn't have time to teach you in undergraduate school.

When our forum ended, we toured the beach house and came upon the wine cabinet displaying all the bottles of wine drunk by teams of astronauts in toasts to each other and their successful missions. Two bottles remained on the shelf unopened, one from the Space Shuttle Challenger's crew and another from Columbia's. It's a sobering moment looking at those two bottles and realize these 14 friends, all comrades on an exciting yet dangerous journey to space, never got a chance to laugh and raise a glass in a toast to their mission's success. They all died tragically, not through any fault of their own, they perished because the engineers and managers, that despite having exceptional skills in mathematics, mechanics, electronics, and computer programming, made catastrophic communication, decision, leadership and ethical mistakes.

When I returned to my office at NASA Headquarters in Washington D.C., my team began developing and implementing our *Fifth Year Program*. The focus of this book is to describe the additional topics we added to our curriculum and share how we developed some very smart newly hired engineers into some of the best all-around engineers in the world.

Earning an undergraduate engineering degree demands an intense amount of focus, work and personal time management and, even upon graduation, the engineering profession requires a commitment to continual technical learning in order to keep pace with the constant advances in science and engineering. Therefore, the logical question becomes, "As an engineer, with a limited amount of time on my hands, do I really need to know about literature, philosophy and the other liberal arts?" Will reading a thousand pages of *Moby Dick* make me a better engineer? What insights does Plato or Socrates have to building a bridge or designing an integrated circuit? How can studying history or astronomy or language make my job easier? These aren't new questions.

It is the hope of this book, and it was the purpose of my career at NASA, to expand and help cultivate the minds of many brilliant engineers, scientists, and technicians. To help them see beyond the equations and the formulas, the design requirements, and the countless, yet critical, system checks that the liberal arts can help them become more successful in their technical careers as well as add a complimentary, and beneficial, aspect to their own complex personalities.

Engineering school was the proverbial *learning through a firehose* experience and, upon graduation, you were placed among kindred engineers, all having a very similar educational experience. In school, our professors had little time, and we had little patience, to study the liberal arts, so it is the purpose of this book to challenge and, hopefully, open your mind to becoming a more well-rounded person and, thus, a better engineer by learning about communication and critical thinking skills, as well as understanding the potent power you possess as an engineer and the personal ethics that must be attentive to such power.

In conclusion, why should an engineer read a 1,000 pages of *Moby Dick*? Because it will help you understand human nature, it will help you understand the world and the audience for whom you design your circuit boards and your skyscrapers. Herman Melville's classic novel will help demonstrate that the real world isn't always numbers and balanced equations and that, even an engineer, must be cognizant of personal, irrational obsessions, be wary of the attraction of strong personalities, and understand how to avoid monumental mistakes by developing critical thinking skills. And it will allow you to appreciate the craftsmanship of a brilliant wordsmith who is able to design his masterpiece with the perfect selection of words that guide the reader's interests and emotions page after page.

Reading the classics like *Moby Dick* just might inspire you to author an e-mail to the chief engineer that demonstrates, not only your technical expertise but also your proficiency to convey that expertise, or a PowerPoint presentation that captivates your audience by thoroughly and skillfully laying out your story, or a white paper for an engineering journal that is erudite as well as comprehensible.

It has been my experience, and pleasure, to work with and learn from numerous scientists, technicians, mathematicians, architects, civil engineers, and so on and in many ways I think we are all kindred spirits—we all want to make our world a better place through technology. The creativity and innovation of STEM professionals are directly responsible for the advancements in technology that fuel our modern-day world and economy and, I believe, the lessons learned in this book apply to all my STEM colleagues.

Although I am an engineer (or engineer-historian?), I originally wrote this book with a technical audience in mind; after all, those are the type of folks I had spent 38 years working with at NASA. In retrospect, and after speaking to a few colleagues who have reviewed this manuscript for me, I believe there's a good bit of value within these pages for many college graduates, despite their major. Feeling free and understanding the importance of speaking up, developing the ability to communicate effectively, developing critical thinking skills, and understanding the necessity for ethical behavior in the workplace are, actually, universal goals and not limited to just science, technology, engineering, and math majors.

This book is made up of four brief chapters (*How We're Made, Communications, Critical Thinking, and Engineering Ethics*) that include numerous case studies, some involving engineering topics, some not. I have purposely kept the four initial chapters short and concise hoping that the reader will learn the most from the following case studies.

Upon reflecting on each case study, it the author's hope that the reader will be able to delineate several lessons from the first four chapters, as each case study holds several examples concerning personality, communications, critical thinking, and ethics.

CHAPTER 1

How We're Made

Typical Design Specifications of an Engineer

A doctor, a priest, and an engineer went golfing. When they came upon the seventh hole, they noticed the two men in front of them were causing a commotion by randomly hitting their golf balls all over the course. As they came upon the two men, the doctor asked if they were OK. The men apologized for causing a disturbance and replied that they were firefighters who had become blinded while saving a puppy from a burning house. They said the country club had awarded them lifetime privileges for their heroism. The doctor replied, "That is amazing, I know some of the best ophthalmologists in the world, I will see if there is something we can do to help you see again." The priest said, "Such unselfish acts of bravery! I will ask my congregation to keep you in their prayers so God can heal you!" Finally, the engineer said, "Why don't you fellas play at night?"

This joke pretty much sums up how many people view an engineer: someone who is logical, practical, and *goal-oriented* to such a degree to be considered somewhat compassionless.

Engineers are generally described, or perhaps stereotyped as:

- Eternally curious, always intrigued to discover how something works
- Relying almost exclusively on logic sometimes to the detriment of emotions and sentimentality
- Making both personal and professional decisions using a cost/benefit analysis. Will the benefits outweigh the costs?

- Possessing an ability to focus and concentrate intently on a topic or problem they find puzzling or interesting
- Preferring order and structure

For most, math is their first language. Math makes an engineer comfortable because it is logical, orderly, absolute, and irrefutable. Math is the international language that everyone, no matter where they're from, understands. Engineers like black and white, they are very uncomfortable when things appear to be gray. There's no debating math.

The famous aerospace engineer, Theodore von Karmon, known as the *father of supersonic flight* once said, "Scientists study the world as it is, engineers create the world that has never been." An engineer takes the laws of physics and using the language of mathematics and his or her own imagination creates useful products and systems. In many ways, an engineer is the unsung hero of modern society. Engineers have a unique power to make dreams come true by turning a concept, an idea, or a hope into reality. Engineers and technical workers all too often take their abilities for granted and seldom realize that, for the non-technical, this skill appears to be almost inexplicable. The skills to build a skyscraper, a computer, or place a man on the moon certainly appear to be magic to the layperson. Just using a smartphone, let alone designing and building one, may be a miraculous accomplishment to most!

Along with these positive attributes that uniquely qualify us to build rockets, construct hydroelectric dams, and design microprocessors we also have complicated characteristics that non-engineers often find confusing and, sometimes, disagreeable:

- Because we focus so intently, many engineers prefer to work alone, which is often misinterpreted as rudeness or even snobbishness to a non-engineer.
- Our reliance on structure and logic can often make us appear dogmatic and unwilling to consider opposing views, especially ones we consider illogical or emotional.
- Because our outlook depends so much on reason to the point where most decisions are made based upon a cost/benefit

analysis, an engineer can often appear cold and impersonal and somewhat indifferent to other people's feelings.
• We prefer to be in a world that is clear-cut and black and white, but in reality, there is no such world.

Peter F. Drucker, the business consultant and author who was instrumental in pushing the management team running General Motors to train their managers in the liberal arts, once wrote: "First-rate engineers, for instance, tend to take pride in not knowing anything about people. Human beings, they believe, are much too disorderly for the good engineering mind."[1]

All these descriptions, both positive and negative, of an engineer's personality also describe the personality trait known as introversion.

Introversion should not be confused with shyness. Shyness is a psychological issue, whereas introversion is a personality type. People who suffer from shyness have deep-seated feelings of apprehension and discomfort when they are around other people and, in certain cases, may require clinical help. Introverts are simply those people who tend to be more comfortable being alone and don't always need external stimulus to be productive.

APPLE's co-founder, Steve Wozniak stated in his autobiography,

[Engineers] … are almost like artists. In fact, the very best of them are artists. And artists work best alone where they can control an invention's design without a lot of other people designing it for marketing or some other committee. I don't believe anything really revolutionary has been invented by committee. If you're that rare engineer who's an inventor and also an artist, I'm going to give you some advice that might be hard to take. That advice is: Work alone. You're going to be best able to design revolutionary products and features if you're working on your own. Not on a committee. Not on a team.[2]

---

[1] P.F. Drucker. 1999. *Managing Oneself.* (Harvard Business Review), p. 3.
[2] S. Wozniak. n.d. *iWoz: Computer Geek to Cult Icon: How I Invented the Personal Computer, Co-Founded Apple, and Had Fun Doing It.*

Although this desire to work alone and a unique ability to focus and logically solve problems can be a huge benefit to an engineer, realize you are also at a disadvantage because the world out there is owned by the non-engineers and the extroverts and, in most cases, they certainly don't understand how you create technological miracles and, at the same time, they really don't understand you.

Extroverts tend to think and act quite differently. For example, while an introvert feels the need for solitude and quiet in order to organize their thoughts, an extrovert needs stimulation and excitement to get their thinking process moving. While an introvert prefers to thoroughly think through every issue before speaking, an extrovert actually speaks first, before thinking. That's how an extrovert's thought process works, they vocalize whatever's on their minds and then think about it.

Life isn't always fair and, as engineers, we have to resign ourselves that we live in an extroverts' world. Like it or not, as Willy Lomar, the aging and tragic salesman in Arthur Miller's classic play, *The Death of a Salesman*, realized, "Personality always wins the day." As an engineer, understand that extroverts tend to have the gregariousness that *wins the day*. After all, even introverts tend to seek out and even align themselves with the extroverted, energized team member. We live in a society, especially in the United States, that admires this and considers charisma to be an essential leadership quality.

Therefore, in order to *win the day* and have a productive and successful career as an engineer in a world of extroverts, you will need to understand you may not be able to change your personality, but you can learn how to adapt. At the appropriate time, you need to be able to transform yourself, at least temporarily, into an *ambivert*.

An ambivert recognizes they are an introvert, and that there's nothing wrong with being one. An ambivert understands the differences he/she may have with extroverted personalities and respects the way an extrovert manages to accomplish their work. An ambivert realizes that in order to be heard, one may have to temporarily shed their introversion and speak up. An ambivert does not have to morph into an extrovert, but an ambivert does need to temporarily fully participate knowing that afterward he/she can re-enter their comfortable world and re-charge their batteries.

There are times when you need to balance the introversion that gives you extraordinary powers of insight and clarity with a more dynamic way of thinking and acting within group settings. If you want to be heard, you have to compete with the extroverts in the room. And there are lots of them.

Elon Musk, the head of SpaceX and Tesla, remarked in an interview with *Business Insider*, "I'm basically like an introverted engineer, so, it took a lot of practice and effort to be able to go up on stage and not just stammer basically... As the CEO, you kind of have to."[3]

For some engineers, it can be quite an enormous effort to speak up and elbow an extrovert off his/her soapbox. But you need to understand, the people around you, the people on your team, and especially your managers *want* to hear what you have to say precisely because you are an introvert. They *know* that when you speak, you've thoroughly thought out the situation and you have something important to contribute. What you say *is* important for them.

Because we live in a world dominated by extroverts, if you don't speak up, some will misinterpret you as holding back your ideas or, worse yet, not having any original ideas.

People want to hear what you have to say, and you have an obligation to your team members, your customers, as well as yourself to be heard. The only way is for you to dial it up and, no matter how uncomfortable you may be, just do it. Stand up and say what you need to say, use hand gestures, and speak loudly and clearly, it's the only way you're going to be heard. No matter how awkward or nervous you may feel, understand that it won't be long before you can have your quiet time, once again, to re-charge your batteries.

As an engineer, you will be assigned to a team and you will need to speak up at meetings and reviews. This isn't always easy, especially for a young engineer intimidated by his or her more experienced team members. Speak up, let your voice be heard, or others will assume you are in agreement. As the Roman poet, Horace, once said, "Silence implies consent." If you're not willing to feel uncomfortable and speak up, then you have no reason to feel neglected or underappreciated.

---

[3] www.forbes.com/sites/carolinecastrillon/2019/01/23/how-introverts-can-thrive -as-entrepreneurs/#127f7f7b5cac.

At NASA, I once had the good fortune to work with a senior project manager who understood that many team members were hesitant to speak up or even ask questions during a meeting with upper management, project scientists, and experienced, lead engineers. He knew many engineers, particularly young ones, feared *looking dumb* when asking a question. So, he took it upon himself to ask the *dumb* questions, just to make sure everyone in the room understood what was being discussed. He fearlessly played devil's advocate with distinguished researchers, forcing them to explain their science in more layman terms. He stopped financial and logistical experts mid-sentence, when he thought the team needed clarification on a budget process or ground support issue. He made certain every engineer left his project meetings with a clear understanding of all the issues discussed and, more importantly, he set the example that there are no dumb questions. From my experience, you won't often find such an understanding, mindful manager, so be prepared to speak up.

Think of it this way: at meetings where you either do not understand or disagree with something said, as a professional, you are ethically required to speak up. Your employer is paying you to participate.

It's important to understand that it's a two-way street for both introverts and extroverts, and you need to show as much understanding to their personality traits as you'd wish they'd show to yours. An extrovert may look at you and think, "Why are you so quiet? If I were that quiet, it would mean I was bored or upset." At the same time, you may look at the extrovert who, in your view, is taking up too much of your precious time talking about non-essential details and think, "Why are you wasting my time?" People are different and for an engineering team to be successful people need to understand each other in order to work effectively together.

So, how does one change (temporarily) from an introvert to an ambivert? There are very few people who relish getting up in front of a group and that can include extroverts, too. One of the world's most popular and iconic singers, Frank Sinatra, once admitted to stage fright, "I swear on my mother's soul, the first four or five seconds, I tremble every time I take the step and I walk out of the wing onto the stage."[4]

---

[4] The Larry King Show. December 26, 1988.

Here's some ways to let your voice be heard:

- Just because you're introverted doesn't mean you don't have passion. Show your passion! This is your project; this is your work, it has your name on it. You've put a lot of thought and effort into it, let it show!
- Practice beforehand. Be alone in a quiet room and talk out loud as if you were before a group. Do it over and over. It's just like anything else, whether it be riding a bike, doing math, writing, or throwing a curveball—it just takes time and practice.
- Imagine yourself succeeding. Picture yourself cool, calm, and collected just as you are when you're among family and friends.
- Look them in the eye but don't single any one person out, spread your vision to briefly include everyone in the audience.
- The audience is on your side, they sincerely want to learn from you, and they genuinely want you to succeed. They do not want to watch you fail; that would be as uncomfortable for them as it would be for you.
- As an engineer, you're probably a perfectionist in some manner but don't worry if you stumble; everyone does. Next time you're in an audience and listening to a speaker, pay attention how many times they stumble and realize that, as an audience member, you generally overlook it and concentrate on the speaker's message.
- Don't be overly concerned that your nervousness is showing. You never outwardly show the same level of nervousness as you feel. You'll notice this if you ever are videotaped during a presentation. You'll be surprised how composed you looked when, at the time, you felt terribly nervous.
- Don't become confused if members of the audience appear to have frowns or are squinting or look as like they might even be displeased. This is the natural look of someone who is concentrating and trying to understand what they are hearing. If they look intent, it means you've gained their interest.

- You're just as qualified as anyone else in the room. Remember Eleanor Roosevelt's quote: "No one can make you feel inferior without your consent."
- Do not wait until you're the last one to speak. This almost guarantees failure because your nerves will be building up to a crescendo by the time you get up there and speak. It might sound contrary, but volunteer to go first, no matter how nervous you might be. You'll actually be at an advantage because you'll gain the audiences' respect, and they'll also tend to be a little more forgiving to the person who volunteers to speak first.
- You're a smart person, you're an engineer after all, share your thoughts, share what you know. Sharing knowledge is what makes engineering teams successful. Remember, "No one lights a lamp and then puts it under a basket. Instead, a lamp is placed on a stand, where it gives light to everyone in the house."[5] Even if you have all the engineering talent in the world, it will go unnoticed and unappreciated unless you speak up and be noticed.

Suggested Resources

Cain, S. 2012. "The Power of Introverts." TED Talk. www.ted.com/talks/susan_cain_the_power_of_introverts.

Cain, S. 2012. "Quiet: The Power of Introverts in a World That Can't Stop Talking." Crown Publishing.

Faw, B. 2014. "Energize Passion and Performance With User Friendly Brain Tools." Aloha Publishing.

Harvey, J.B. 1988. *The Abilene Paradox and Other Meditations on Management.* Jossey-Bass Publisher.

Website: How Does Your Personality Type Affect Your Income? www.visualcapitalist.com/myers-briggs-personality-income/.

Website: Introvert, Dear. https://introvertdear.com.

---

[5] New Living Translation, Matthew 5:15.

Case Study: An Engineer's Remorse

Regret for things we did is tempered by time but regret for things we did not do is inconsolable.

—Sydney J. Harris

The NASA Challenger tragedy holds many lessons for engineers and managers. Not only did we lose seven astronauts, but such a horrific tragedy affected all those involved during the launch. If ever there was a lesson learned for engineers about communication and speaking up, it was the Challenger accident.

On the morning of January 28, 1986, as NASA prepared to launch the Space Shuttle Challenger, a group of Morton Thiokol engineers responsible for the solid rocket boosters unanimously recommended against launching due to the record cold weather the evening before at the Kennedy Space Center. Temperatures had dropped well below 20°F that night and were still near freezing the morning of the launch. Prelaunch inspections relayed to management that ice was still present all around the pad. Never before had a shuttle launched in such cold weather.

Shuttle team experts had been aware from the start of the program that the solid rocket motors strapped to the sides of the shuttle's main fuel tank had an inadequate O-ring joint design and had seen evidence from previous launches that the internal O-rings had shown evidence of burn-through. These experts also understood that the cold weather would exasperate the problem by making the O-rings stiff and brittle and susceptible to cracking.

In order to get the necessary funding for the shuttle program, the space agency had promised the American people that space flight was going to be routine but on January 28, after numerous technical delays, NASA managers were under extreme pressure to get the shuttle into orbit.

Aboard this shuttle flight was Christa McAuliffe, America's teacher in space. While in orbit, she was going to engage and transmit to thousands of schoolchildren on earth numerous science lessons and also prove that space flight was no longer the reserve of those military pilots possessing the *right stuff*. Christa McAuliffe was NASA's proof that the shuttle was making spaceflight routine.

As the countdown proceeded, the Morton Thiokol engineers discussed their concerns with the O-ring joint and the cold weather with NASA managers. Eventually, NASA forced Morton Thiokol managers to override the concerns of their dissenting engineers—the experts on solid rocket boosters—who had presented convincing evidence that the O-ring joint may fail.

Challenger launched and, of course, disintegrated 73 seconds into its flight.

Bob Ebeling, one of the dissenting Morton Thiokol engineers who tried to convince his own managers and NASA not to launch, never got over the tragedy. For the rest of his life, he was haunted by the accident and his role in it. He wondered if he could have tried harder to argue against the launch, perhaps he could have explained his data more clearly or more forcefully. Years later, he told an interviewer, "I think that was one of the mistakes God made. He shouldn't have picked me for that job. I don't know. But next time I talk to him, I'm going to ask him, why me? You picked a loser."[6]

---

[6] www.npr.org/templates/transcript/transcript.php?storyId=464744781.

Case Study: A Hypersonic Visit to Abilene

Early in my career at NASA, one of the first training sessions I took as an apprentice mechanic featured a short movie called *The Abilene Complex*. Over the years, I attended countless training sessions, but the story of this simple 15-minute movie stuck with me throughout my career.

The original author of the Abilene Complex was Dr. Jerry B. Harvey, a management consultant and author. It's based on a real-life situation he found himself in while visiting his in-laws in Coleman, Texas, during the early 1970s.

The story, at least the way I remember it, goes like this…

Jerry and his wife spent the morning driving through Texas to visit his wife's parents. By mid-afternoon, Jerry, his wife, and mother-in-law were playing a game of dominoes on the front porch. Although it was a stifling hot Texas afternoon, they were enjoying a breeze while sipping lemonade. The three of them were laughing about some old family stories when his father-in-law came out to join them and asked if they'd like to take a ride out to Abilene for dinner.

Jerry felt a bit hesitant because he was really relaxed and was enjoying himself but, being a guest at his in-laws *home*, he didn't want to appear rude. He replied, "I guess so, sure, if everyone else is up for it." His wife, Pat, a bit surprised that Jerry wanted to go for another long car ride after spending hours driving to Coleman, said, "Jerry's never been to Abilene, this ought to be fun!" And finally, his mother-in-law, who had been planning to cook a nice dinner for her family but did not want to disappoint the couple who seemed interested in restaurant in Abilene said, "That sounds great! I always look forward to getting out of the kitchen for an evening."

The dominoes were put back in their box, the pitcher of lemonade was placed in the refrigerator and, as they got into the car, Jerry's father-in-law mentioned that they need to keep the windows rolled down because his air conditioning has been on the blink.

Abilene is about 50 miles from Coleman. When they finally arrived, the dust from the Texas roads felt as if it had been coated to their sweaty skin. The restaurant was very crowded and, once served, their food was barely appetizing. Then they got back in the car for the long, hot, dusty, quiet ride home.

Once home, everyone dusted off their clothes and wearily sat down on the porch, hoping the evening breeze would pick up to cool them down.

Jerry's mother-in-law brought out the pitcher of lemonade and said, "Well, wasn't that fun!" That's when the fireworks started to go off. Jerry's wife replied, "Are you kidding? We were having a wonderful time playing dominoes and now I'm exhausted, caked in dust, and still hungry!"

Mother-in law: Well, I wanted to cook you a nice dinner but you insisted on going to Abilene!

Jerry's wife: I only wanted to go because Jerry seemed so excited about seeing Abilene!

Jerry: Wait a minute! I drove all morning to get here. The last thing in the world I wanted to do was get back into a car—one without air conditioning—and go for another drive! I was enjoying myself beating both of you at dominoes!

Father-in-law: Yea, actually, I was looking forward to mom's home cookin'. Been there before and I never cared for that restaurant.

This is the point when all hell broke loose. Jerry, his wife, and his mother-in-law all gang up on his father-in-law.

Mother-in-law: What? You got to be kidding! It was all your idea! None of us wanted to go to Abilene!

Jerry's wife: Dad, we drove out here to spend time with you and mom. You're the one who insisted we go to Abilene.

Father-in-law: I just wanted to make sure you guys were enjoying your visit. Y'all looked so bored out on the porch. Jerry seemed to jump at the chance to visit Abilene and everyone quickly agreed. Don't blame me!

Jerry: Wiping the sweat from his brow, Oh God… Listen, I just wanted to do what the group wanted. I'm a guest here. Dad sounded like it would be a fun trip, and I wasn't about to interfere with everyone's plans. How is it that we unanimously agreed to do something none of us wanted to do?

The family debate ended without a clear consensus, and they all decided it was time to wash off the crusted dust and grime from their faces and get some sleep.

Later in in my career, after I became an engineer, one of my first projects involved manufacturing a new *diluent injection flange* (DIF) for NASA's Hypersonic Test Facility (HTF).[7] The HTF was built during the late 1960s to test rocket motors, missiles, and perform research on scramjet applications. Hypersonic test tunnels can create wind speeds between Mach 4 and Mach 7, and most utilize the exhaust from a device like a turbine engine to simulate such high air speeds. Although the exhaust gas can provide accurate aerodynamic flow conditions on a test object, the air stream is contaminated with combustion gasses and heat and does not reflect the real-world conditions of a device flying in the atmosphere at those speeds. The HTF is one of the few hypersonic tunnels in the world that is capable of simulating the true temperature, altitude, and atmospheric conditions that an object flying hypersonically would encounter.

To accomplish this, gaseous nitrogen is heated to 4,000°F and pressurized to 1,200 psig within an enormous pressure vessel. In line with the vessel is a large radiation valve, and when this is opened, the heated stream of nitrogen passes through the valve and into the DIF, which then injects the appropriate combination of oxygen and nitrogen (the diluent) into the airstream, which then passes into the test chamber simulating real-world test conditions on the model.

The HTF pushes the boundaries of engineering design, and the diluent flange, in particular, operates at the extreme edge for materials. In 1996, an O-ring sealing the radiation valve to the DIF failed, and as the hot gas escaped through the O-ring joint, it began to vaporize the radiation valve, which subsequently damaged the DIF. The radiation valve was completely destroyed, forcing NASA to fabricate an entirely new one while hoping to repair the DIF, but after several attempts, it became evident the only solution would be to manufacture a new DIF, as well.

---

[7] The HTF is a fascinating engineering achievement and one of many national engineering treasures maintained by NASA. More can be learned here: www1 .grc.nasa.gov/facilities/htf/.

The material required to build a new DIF was the same used to manufacture the radiation valve: SA-302 Grade B Carbon Steel, an obscure type of steel that could withstand extreme temperatures and pressures but was also very difficult to machine and weld because of its high molybdenum content. Because it was so infrequently used in industry, it was very expensive, and when it was ordered, NASA was required to purchase an entire mill run, 70,000 pounds, much more than was needed for the 2,500-pound radiation valve. Plus, the steel ordered for the radiation valve was 7 in. thick, which was the final dimension for the DIF, meaning there would be no room for any machining or welding errors if we used the leftover SA-302 Grade B on the DIF.

I was a young manufacturing engineer on the team assigned to fabricate the new DIF. Because the Department of Defense had an immediate need to use the HTF, we were given the fast track to get our job done, and NASA assigned a lead engineer who was one of the most prominent designers within the agency and who had also been part of the original team when the HTF was built. The rest of our team consisted of a metallurgist, a CAD programmer, a procurement specialist, a welder, and several machinists.

To fabricate the radiation valve, NASA ordered the required 7-in.-thick plates of SA-302 Grade B but now we faced a critical decision: do we try to use the leftover 302 Grade B from the radiation valve, or do we go to the expense and order a whole new mill run of slightly thicker SA-302 Grade B?

During one of our initial meetings, we briefly discussed the difficulties we might encounter fabricating the 4-ft. diameter, 1,800-pound DIF with the undersized steel left over from the radiation valve, but our procurement specialist, who was primarily concerned with cost, advocated that we avoid purchasing more steel and "use your engineering know-how, technical skills, and creativity" to build the DIF with the leftover material. Each of us on the technical side had concerns but agreed to move forward using the leftover steel.

After six stressful and grueling months of trying to manufacture a new DIF, the effort was scrapped, and new, thicker steel was ordered. Even the best machinists in the world couldn't avoid the laws of physics. The leftover steel from the radiation valve didn't provide enough thickness to allow for even the slightest machining imperfection, and it warped when the required welds were performed.

Afterward, our division had initiated a post-project assessment modeled after the U.S. Army's *After Action Review* to document lessons learned. As the manufacturing engineer, I led the review.

Lead engineer:	I wanted to order new steel of the appropriate size right from the beginning. We already had plenty of engineering issues that needed to be worked out. Why make it even harder using the wrong size material?
Metallurgist:	I thought we should look at other steels, many new, stronger, cheaper alloys have been developed since the original DIF was made.
Lead machinist:	I knew this was going to be a disaster from the get-go. It always happens this way, engineers never ask the advice of the folks that actually have to make their screwed-up designs.
Procurement specialist:	Why didn't you all tell me it was impossible to make this out of the leftover steel? Now we've wasted six months, and it's going to cost us twice as much to make!

This is the part of the meeting where all hell broke loose.

Red-faced, depressed manufacturing engineer: "Oh God… Listen, I just wanted to do what the group recommended. I considered all of you experts. You all sounded like it was doable, and I wasn't about to interfere. How is it that we unanimously agreed to do something none of us wanted to do?"

Questions to Consider

- Have you ever found yourself in a similar situation as Jerry did? Are there ways to speak up and effectively communicate your feelings without appearing rude? Some people have a knack for talking their way out of tough situations, while others resort to being blunt to the point of rudeness. What could Jim have said to diplomatically get out of the ride to Abilene?

- Jerry was faced with a predicament. He really didn't want to go to Abilene. Could he explain his feelings in a judicious manner to avoid hurting his father-in-law's feelings? What if he couldn't politely explain his desire not to go to Abilene and ended up appearing rude? Would that have also spoiled the family's evening?

- Sometimes it's easier to express a dissenting opinion among work colleagues than it is with family members. After all, it's business, and in a business environment, most people understand logic, reason, and the *bottom line* take precedence over hurt feelings. Upon reflection, when I was a young, inexperienced engineer chairing our initial manufacturing meeting to discuss using the leftover material for the DIF, I wanted to make a good impression with the folks I was going to lead, and I also felt a bit insecure challenging experts. What would have been a more appropriate tactic?

Case Study: Herbert Hoover and the Limits of Intelligence

At one time, he was considered the most admired, and perhaps the smartest man in the world. He was credited with saving an entire nation from starving in the midst of the Great War. In an era of industrial innovation, such as radio and commercial aviation, he used his masterful organizational skills to efficiently regulate new markets, allowing these modern miracles to flourish in the marketplace and become available to almost everyone in America. He forced state governments, who had bickered for decades over water rights along the Colorado River, to compromise and build a dam that brought untold wealth and prosperity where none had existed. He was born poor, and soon became an orphan, but against all odds, through hard work and determination, he made his way through Stanford, eventually earning millions as a mining engineer.

By all accounts, Herbert Hoover was a brilliant man whose stunning successes early in his career should have paved the way for what both Democrats and Republicans thought would be a triumphant presidency, ushering in affluence and prosperity with a publicly declared goal of ending poverty in America. He was elected president by one of the biggest landslides in American history. Four years later, he was thrown out of office by the same electorate, who now viewed him as one of the most reviled men in America. For decades, rather than being honored for his achievements, his name would be synonymous with failure.

Hoover's tragic fall from grace can obviously be traced to the economic crash of 1929 that left over a quarter of the American workforce unemployed. As the president desperately tried to address the crisis, his engineering personality—the one that had made him so successful in the past—was now, perhaps, the primary reason for his legendary fall.

The Belgian Relief

In the late summer of 1914, the German Army unleashed its forces through the neutral country of Belgium on their way to the French frontier. At war with both Russia to the east and France to the west, German military planners had seen the route through Belgium as the only way to avoid a war on two fronts. The plan was to quickly defeat the French, then move their armies eastward to defeat the slowly mobilizing Russian army. But the Germans miscalculated horribly, and their assault on neutral Belgium brought Great Britain into the war, which, in turn, prevented any prospect for a quick victory in France. For the next four years, the German Army would occupy Belgium as war raged throughout Europe.

Great Britain's biggest asset was its navy, and they immediately began a blockade of the entire European continent in an effort to starve Germany. The blockade included Belgium, because the English considered it Germany's responsibility to feed the countries it overran. The German response, in this most merciless of wars, was to escalate stakes even further by introducing submarine warfare to starve the British.

Public outrage at seeing the neutral Belgians caught in a vise of starvation caused the British and American governments to look for a solution. Herbert Hoover, the 40-year-old American mining engineer, was living in London during these frantic and terrifying days as the Germans moved toward Paris. Thousands of American tourists and nationals streamed from the continent to London, seeking safety and hoping to return home. Hoover helped organize a relief effort providing food, shelter, and eventually funds for their safe return to the States.

After graduating in the initial class of Stanford, Hoover spent years working in Australia, China, and Russia with mining companies where he was known for his obsession with increasing efficiencies and had been described by a fellow mining engineer, "…we may say there is no cleverer engineer in the two hemispheres."[8] By the time he had settled in London, he had invested his earnings and had a successful consulting business and was, perhaps, the wealthiest and most well-known engineer in the world. But now he had sensed a higher purpose, confiding to friends that he, "…was as rich as any man has a right to be," adding, "…just making money isn't enough."[9] Hoover wanted to enter public service and, "get

---

[8] W.E. Leuchtenburg. n.d. *Herbert Hoover* (Library of Congress), http://catdir.loc.gov/catdir/enhancements/fy1113/2008026456-s.html.

[9] H. Hoover. n.d. *The Ordeal of Woodrow Wilson*, Preface by Sen. Mark Hatfield, p. 16.

Figure 1.1 Herbert Hoover, soon after his graduation from Stanford
Source: Herbert Hoover Presidential Library.

into the big game somewhere."[10] As the Belgian disaster unfolded, the American ambassador in London, having witnessed his humanitarianism and acute ability to organize, thought Hoover might be the key to saving seven million Belgians.

Hoover took charge. He negotiated with the English to allow passage through the blockade and with the Germans to allow distribution networks throughout Belgium, along with promises the food would not be taken from civilians and distributed to the army. In 1914, most people thought the war would be over in a few months, but the Great War dragged on for four savage years. Throughout this desperate time, Hoover's Commission for the Relief of Belgium raised almost a billion dollars in relief funds and operated so efficiently that less than one half of 1 percent was used for overhead. Throughout the war, Hoover refused any

---

[10] G.H. Nash. 1874–1914. *The Life of Herbert Hoover* (The Engineer), pp. 509–513.

salary and paid his own expenses.[11] Within Belgium and northern France, the commission fed over nine million people a day and food distribution areas became known as *Hoover restaurants*. To this day, numerous streets and boulevards as well as statues of Hoover mark the area.

At the war's end, President Wilson, a Democrat and Progressive, appointed Hoover as Food Administrator to coordinate production of the nation's farms. In 1919, Hoover founded the *American Relief Administration* (ARA) where he sought to repeat his miracle in Belgium to help feed millions of starving people throughout war-torn Europe. The ARA was funded with 100 million dollars by Congress, and Hoover raised another 100 million in donations throughout America. To realize the level of devastation caused by the Great War, the ARA was shipping food to Europe up until 1922—five years after hostilities ended.

In 1921, the long-suffering people of Russia—now the Soviet Union—who had endured catastrophic losses in the war and withstood two revolutions and a bloody civil war, were now facing famine. Few in the west, and particularly Hoover, trusted the Soviets, yet the American Congress appropriated 20 million dollars in humanitarian relief earmarked for the Soviet famine, and Hoover set in motion his machinery to feed over 10.5 million Russians per day.[12] Displaying a gratitude stretching across political boundaries, Maxim Gorky, the Soviet writer of international repute, wrote Hoover, "In the past year you have saved from death three and one-half million children, five and one-half million adults... I know of no accomplishment which in ... magnitude and generosity can be compared to the relief that you actually accomplished."[13]

By this time, Herbert Hoover was a household name, not just in America but throughout the world. He had earned the nickname *The*

---

[11] H. Hoover. 1928. *Master of Emergencies*, 1928 documentary, www.youtube.com/watch?v=d12XBYFmGWE.

[12] The Russian relief effort ended in 1923 when it was discovered the Soviet government had begun exporting wheat to bring in desperately needed foreign capital. George Keenan, the American diplomat and *cold warrior* believed Hoover's humanitarianism had backfired and helped keep the Soviets in power during these trying times facing the incipient regime.

[13] W.E. Leuchtenburg. n.d. *Herbert Hoover: The American Presidents Series: The 31st President, 1929-1933*, p. 58.

Great Engineer. He was courted by both parties and, with the democrats' prospects so weak, there was a push within the party for a Herbert Hoover–Franklin D. Roosevelt ticket in 1920. The ambitious and shrewd Roosevelt was enthusiastic at the possibility of riding Hoover's successes to national office and responded, "Hoover is certainly a wonder. I wish I could make him president of the United States. There could not be a better one."[14] But Hoover chose the Republicans, and in 1921, was appointed by newly elected President Harding as Secretary of Commerce.

Herbert Hoover brought his boundless energy to the Commerce Department and turned the previously unknown little agency into a vibrant new organization that quickly began to transform the American landscape.[15] Hoover reversed the adversarial relationships that past administrations had had with business and sought to create a partnership where government could help streamline regulations and develop standards to help American businesses become more efficient in the international marketplace.

Hoover relentlessly pursued ways to make the government, American industry, and consumers more efficient, and enacted institutional changes that we are still benefiting from today. In the nascent age of radio, Hoover realized the need for government ownership of the airwaves to regulate and organize the already-confusing and inefficient system in place. He worked with Congress to establish the Federal Radio Commission (now known as the Federal Communications Commission).

He energized the almost-forgotten Bureau of Standards so that it could help industry by simplifying the manufacturing processes, warehousing inventories, and distributing goods by standardizing products. With the Bureau, Hoover looked for efficiencies everywhere throughout the economy and had millions of consumer and industrial products tested. The *Great Engineer* was dumbfounded at the inefficiencies and waste throughout American industry. For example, he discovered American manufacturers were making

---

[14] J.E. Smith. n.d. *FDR*, p. 177.

[15] Hoover began work on a gargantuan new building for the Department of Commerce on Constitution Avenue that, upon completion in 1932, was the largest office building in the world. In 1981, Senator Mark Hatfield, who, as a young graduate student at Stanford, had been a protégé of the retired president, submitted legislation to have the building renamed, *The Herbert C. Hoover Building*.

66 different sizes of paving stones, even though the market primarily pur-chased just five basic sizes of bricks. Making so many different styles, most of which went unused, caused huge extra costs in inventories, molds, handling, and shipping—costs that were all passed on to the consumer.

Hoover's Commerce Department didn't stop there. They set standards that limited the number of redundant sizes and styles of products being wastefully manufactured, including nails and tacks (428 different sizes were being produced), shovels (there were 4,460 different varieties), bolts (1,500 different varieties were being manufactured[16]), sheet steel (1,819 different sizes and gages were being pressed), hand files and rasps (1,351 different styles were manufactured), woven wire fence (552 different styles were being sold), hot water tanks (120 different tank sizes), sink plumbing traps (1,114 different sizes and varieties), paint brushes (480 different styles), and milk bottles (49 different sizes and shapes). These were just a few of the items being manufactured by industry that Hoover used his engineering skills to simplify and make more efficient.[17]

Under Hoover's direction, the Commerce Department combed the entire economy, looking for areas that would benefit from standardiza-tion. Men's hats were made in over 3,486 different styles, grades, sizes, and colors; after Hoover met with hat manufacturers, they were able to streamline this burdensome production effort to 600 varieties, thus not only allowing smaller factory inventories but also retailer inventories. They limited men's' shoes from 2,500 different styles in each of three grades to 100 different styles with just a single grade.

National Politics: The Great Engineer Leaves His Comfort Zone

In 1928, Calvin Coolidge shocked most Americans by refusing to run for a second term. Few of the hardline Republican party bosses who,

---

[16] Consider a small hardware store in rural America that had to stock, or try to locate, over 1,500 different bolts for various tractors, farm equipment, automo-biles, and so on.

[17] E. Triebel. n.d. *The Department of Commerce Under Herbert Hoover 1921–1928*, p. 72.

like Coolidge, lived by the unwavering doctrine of small government, fully trusted Hoover, but all could see his nomination was as unstoppable. Upon accepting the nomination of his party, Hoover displayed his progressive side by promising to create a Farm Board that would, "…establish for our farmers an income equal to those of other occupations." Four months later, the new president backed up his words by granting the Board a 500-million-dollar budget and stated, "I invest you with responsibilities and resources such as have never before been conferred by our government in assistance to any industry."

Hoover went on to win the presidency by a landslide, beating the Democrat, Al Smith, with a staggering 58 percent of the popular vote.

Hoover ended his inauguration speech by saying, "I have no fears for the future of our country. It is bright with hope." The new president didn't realize that a decade of huge industrial growth was about to burst due to free-falling commodity prices and uncontrolled speculative trading on Wall Street. His talk of *hope* was about to haunt him forever.

Eight months after Hoover took office, the stock market crashed, ushering in the Great Depression. If anyone in American history was in the wrong place at the wrong time, it was Herbert Hoover. This was an unprecedented event in human history, and no one had any idea how to stop it.

The Great Depression was staggering in its catastrophic economic enormity. In the four years Hoover served as president, industrial production fell by more than one half. Stock prices lost 90 percent of their value, wiping out savings for millions of Americans while their disposable income dropped nearly a third. One out of four Americans were out of work—almost 13 million men.[18][19] The American stock market would not recoup the losses of 1929 until 25 years later in 1954.

Hoover disregarded the counsel of his own Secretary of the Treasury, Andrew Mellon, who, having been in office through both Harding's and

---

[18] L.W. Reed. n.d. *Great Myths of the Great Depression* (Foundation for Economic Education), https://fee.org/resources/great-myths-of-the-great-depression-pdf-and-audio/.

[19] Women would not become a major part of the American workforce until the Second World War. Therefore, if 13 million men were out of work, this means 13 million families without an income.

Figure 1.2 President Hoover posing with his dog, King Tut
Source: U.S. National Archives.

Coolidge's presidencies, and presided over the greatest economic boon in American history, advised the president that this was an overdue slump in the economy and, although there would be temporary pain, market forces would make the natural corrections.

But Hoover was an engineer, after all, and believed if something was broken, there must be a way to fix it. He met with industrial and business leaders, urging them to ignore basic economic laws and insisted they avoid layoffs or even cut employees' wages, despite the loss of demand and the resultant glut of available workers. Out of principle, he still refused to use federal dollars for public relief and welfare. The president preferred to get people back to work rather than see them grow dependent upon handouts, and so he urged the states to increase public works while also increasing federal projects, such as the Hoover Dam.

Hoover's Farm Board now tried to help farmers by purchasing their goods at above-market prices, only to discover this became an incentive for farmers to grow more, which added to their misery by resulting in unwanted surpluses that drove the price of their goods even lower on the free market.

Desperately trying to stem rising unemployment, Hoover authorized the expulsion of over half a million migrant workers back to Mexico in hopes unemployed Americans would fill their jobs.

By 1932, thousands of businesses were failing, and as many farms were falling under foreclosure, Hoover opened the Reconstruction Finance Corporation that provided loans to banks, railroads, and other businesses in hopes of stimulating the economy.

Also, in 1932, the president signed the Emergency Relief and Construction Act that provided funding for public works and, for the first time, loans to private construction companies to build low-cost housing for the poor.

On February 27, 1932, President Hoover signed the Glass–Steagall Act that enhanced the powers of the Federal Reserve. This, first step, would later become much more formidable under FDR as it became an effort to reform banking and greatly restrict the types of investments banks were permitted to make.

In Hoover's engineering mind, an equation must be balanced, so he was convinced this unprecedented foray into huge federal spending also required a balanced budget to pay for it. With the Revenue Act of 1932, he raised taxes across the board on all Americans. He believed doing so was necessary to keep the federal government solvent, but instead, it added more fuel to a crisis that was simply burning out of control. "At the end of 1931, President Herbert Hoover asked for a temporary tax increase, saying it was 'indispensable to the restoration of confidence.' Congress went along in June 1932, raising the top income tax rate from 25 percent to 63 percent and quadrupling the lowest tax rate from 1.1 percent to 4 percent. That didn't help confidence or the Treasury. Revenue from the individual income tax dropped from $834 million in 1931 to $427 million in 1932 and $353 million in 1933."[20]

---

[20] A. Reynolds. September 29, 2008. *Forbes Magazine*, www.forbes.com/2008 /09/28/hoover-congress-schumer-oped-cx_ar_0928reynolds.html.

But the worst *fix* Hoover attempted on the American economy was undoubtedly the Smoot–Hawley Tariff Act. In an attempt to protect American companies and farmers, the president raised tariffs on almost all imported goods. This produced the opposite effect than intended, as other nations retaliated and raised tariffs on American goods, thus compounding the problem at home and spreading the depression overseas.[21] Over a 1,000 American economists sent a petition to Hoover pleading him to veto the measure.

After all his efforts, Hoover entered the 1932 elections with an economy still in free-fall, a desperate population, and an opponent whose style and political shrewdness he simply could not match.

As the election neared, Roosevelt, a career politician who understood how elections and politics worked, attempted to broaden his base, addressing voters who had previously supported Republicans by painting his opponent as a big government candidate and accusing Hoover of not only "…reckless and extravagant spending," but also taking the power of local and state governments and concentrating, "…control of everything in Washington as rapidly as possible." He further blamed Hoover for presiding over the "…greatest spending administration in peacetime in all of history." FDR's running mate, John Nance Garner, incredibly accused Hoover of "…leading the country down the path of socialism."[22]

FDR, in an interview with the *New York Times*, dismissed the aura of *The Great Engineer* by stating, "The Presidency … is more than an engineering job, efficient or inefficient. It is pre-eminently a place of moral leadership."[23] Roosevelt assured his interviewer that *he* was no engineer,[24] and that he was going to apply, "simple rules of human conduct"[25] as president.

---

[21] Some historians go as far as blaming the Smoot–Hawley tariff for increasing economic chaos in Europe and setting the stage for extremists such as Hitler.

[22] L.W. Reed. n.d. *The Greatest Spending Administration in all of History*, www .mackinac.org/4026.

[23] *The New York Times Magazine*. September 11, 1932, p. 2.

[24] A. Shlaes. n.d. *The Forgotten Man*, p. 134.

[25] *The New York Times Magazine*. September 11, 1932, p. 2.

Rather than the dull and seemingly endless monologues that characterized the Hoover campaign, FDR understood how to win over people, even a nation desperate for hope, by running an optimistic campaign, even choosing, *Happy Days Are Here Again* as his campaign song. Roosevelt was outgoing and charming and loved mixing with crowds. He was an extraordinarily polished speaker who knew exactly how to change the mood of an audience to suit his purpose. By contrast, President Hoover was almost the exact opposite. Although intensely focused and industrious with impeccable personal integrity, he was seldom comfortable around people and could be awkward at large social or press events. Hoover didn't work his way up the ladder through politics to become president—the presidency was his first and only experience as a politician, and he never understood the lying, the deal-making, and the personal attacks that are inherent to politics. Herbert Hoover was a man from the world of engineering lost and confused in the world of politics.

As the election neared, the president firmly believed the American people would recognize his history of hard work, his honesty, and his intelligence, and re-elect him to a second term. He was stunned when the electorate voted Franklin Roosevelt into office by an even larger landslide than Hoover had won in 1929.

Now FDR and his New Deal were in charge, and the Great Depression was their problem. Roosevelt followed the direction that Hoover had set, but after seeing little progress, he began implementing even more radical plans. Rexford Tugwell, an economist and part of FDR's *Brain Trust* that was gathered to deal with the economy, later wrote: "When it was all over, I once made a list of New Deal ventures begun during Hoover's years as secretary of commerce and then as president.... The New Deal owed much to what he had begun."[26] But in the end, it was the Second World War that pulled America out of the worst economic collapse in history.

Both men had learned to loathe each other. When Hoover and FDR shared the traditional open car ride to the inauguration ceremony, both men looked uncomfortable as they passed the crowds, and neither

---

[26] T. McNeese and R. Jensen. n.d. *The Great Depression 1929–1938*, p. 43.

spoke the entire ride. For the rest of his life, Hoover would never visit Washington if Roosevelt was in town. He never wanted to be caught in a situation where he'd have to see him again.

The mutual enmity never ended. Hoover, greatly annoying Roosevelt, spent years on the speaker circuit warning about the radicalism of the New Deal and later writing countless essays and books claiming FDR was endangering the nation with a foolish foreign policy that would inevitably lead to another world war. For their part, Roosevelt and his team of New Dealers completely understood how political machinations worked, and so Hoover became their doormat as they relentlessly manipulated public opinion and cleverly twisted the history of Hoover's years as president by blaming him for a depression that went on unabated for two more of FDR's four elected terms.[27] History is written by the victors, and this account of the Hoover presidency still resonates today in most history books and classrooms.

Logic and Reason Don't Always Sell

Herbert Hoover's life was a testament to the values of hard work, rugged individualism, taking advantage of opportunities, and personal responsibility—qualities that proved invaluable to his success. In retrospect, it's ironic that a man like Hoover, who worked his way through poverty to become wealthy and gave it all up for public service, a humanitarian who fed and saved millions of lives, would be known as uncaring and unsympathetic to peoples' misfortunes during the Great Depression. What may be even more ironic is how Franklin Roosevelt, a man born

---

[27] The Hoover Dam is a good example of this animus. As Secretary of Commerce, Hoover had finally convinced the southwestern states into an agreement about water flow of the Colorado River enabling the construction of, at the time, the world's largest dam. During his presidency it was officially named *The Hoover Dam* by his secretary of the interior. At the time, this was not unusual, FDR would name numerous dams and public works after sitting senators and public servants in order to get their support. When the Roosevelt administration took over, the dam was quickly renamed *The Boulder Dam*. In 1947, the Congress officially restored the name as *The Hoover Dam*.

into a wealthy American aristocratic family, would be seen as a champion of the poor.

Hoover did have a *soft side*, which he hid from the press and the public. During the worst days of the Great Depression, in order to get away from the stress, infighting, and heat of Washington, he built a small cabin in the Blue Ridge Mountains where he would do what he loved best: fly-fishing. In this secluded area of Appalachia, he met the desperately poor and built the children in this area their first schoolhouse. He would relax and spend time with the locals, most of who were already so impoverished that the depression meant little to them, chatting around a fire.

Hoover's personality had a lot to do with his fall. Maybe FDR was right: engineers don't necessarily make great presidents. Herbert Hoover proved that *the smartest man in the room* doesn't necessarily make the best leader, especially without an aptitude for dealing in the fiercely competitive and rancorous world of politics.

Hoover was fixated on engineering principles—rules that worked perfectly in the workshop and laboratory but failed miserably in the complex world of people and politics. A good example is Hoover's obsession with efficiency. Sometimes there are parts of life that demand inefficiency when people are involved. Sometimes it pays to waste time, and money, getting to know someone, learning to understand someone.

When Hoover would get an idea or a sudden inspiration, he was known to walk out of a room while someone was still speaking to him. He could appear cold to some. Gutzon Borglum, the sculptor of Mt Rushmore, visited Hoover looking for funding and once said, "If you put a rose in Hoover's hand, it would wilt."[28]

Engineering precision was in every facet of Hoover's makeup. "Hoover ... often wrote as if composing a legal brief. He was after accuracy, not color, with the result that he unintentionally bleached much of the color of daily life and individual character from his laboriously composed pages."[29]

---

[28] www.duncanentertainment.com/alter.php.

[29] H. Hoover. n.d. *The Ordeal of Woodrow Wilson*, Preface by Sen (Mark Hatfield), p. 9.

An engineer deals in a black and white world: something either works or it doesn't. If it doesn't, there must be a logical, fixable cause. At times, the engineer's personality seems to mimic the system he or she is attempting to troubleshoot—completely logical and void of emotion. If there's high resistance, replace the faulty resistor; low airflow, replace the filter; and all is well again. But life isn't black and white, and politics and leadership often demand such illogical feelings as compassion, sympathy, and warmth.

Outside the comfortable technical realm of the engineer lies chaos. It's an incomprehensible world where 2 + 2 sometimes does not equal 4. It's a world where an engineer's intelligence and experience sometimes counts very little, and can even count against them. As Jonathon Alter said,

> Hoover was not very convincing when he would talk. His own aides tried to get him to be less boring. He would read, literally, 50-page speeches in a monotone. You can't lead that way, and when he would be told, can you try to lighten up? Can you try to even just look up more when you speak, or look in this direction? He couldn't do it. So, he had these great skills; he was probably one of the three or four brightest American Presidents in terms of his IQ, but in terms of what they call EQ, his emotional intelligence, his ability to relate to people, and to intuit what they were thinking and respond to them, he was in the bottom group.[30]

An Unfair Legacy

In his memoirs, Herbert Hoover, a man who had started with nothing and rose to the presidency only to be pushed aside as a failure by the countrymen he had tried so hard to help, reflected on the profession he loved so much. Sounding nostalgic for a less complicated time, perhaps he finally understood the dichotomy between engineering and the real world:

---

[30] Interview with Jonathan Alter, www.duncanentertainment.com/alter.php.

The great liability of the engineer compared to men of other professions is that his works are out in the open where all can see them... He cannot bury his mistakes in the grave like the doctors. He cannot argue them into thin air or blame the judge like the lawyers. He cannot, like the architects, cover his failures with trees and vines. He cannot, like the politicians, screen his shortcomings by blaming his opponents and hope the people will forget. The engineer simply cannot deny he did it. If his works do not work, he is damned....

On the other hand, unlike the doctor his is not a life among the weak. Unlike the soldier, destruction is not his purpose. Unlike the lawyer, quarrels are not his daily bread. To the engineer falls the job of clothing the bare bones of science with life, comfort, and hope. No doubt as years go by the people forget which engineer did it, even if they ever knew. Or some politician puts his name on it. Or they credit it to some promoter who used other people's money . . . But the engineer himself looks back at the unending stream of goodness which flows from his successes with satisfactions that few professions may know. And the verdict of his fellow professionals is all the accolade he wants.[31]

For decades after he lost to FDR, Hoover had attempted to become, once again, relevant in American politics. Finally, in 1945, when Europe once again lay in waste, an unlikely invitation from President Harry Truman arrived on Hoover's desk, asking his help in feeding the war-torn continent. Truman later enlisted Hoover's help in reorganizing the federal bureaucracy to become more efficient. Truman eventually said, "I feel that I am one of his closest friends and he is one of my closest friends."[32]

Herbert Hoover, *The Great Engineer*, lived until 1963 when he passed away at 90 years of age. The *New York Times* obituary read, "He fed more people and saved more lives than any other man in history."[33]

---

[31] H. Hoover. 1954. "Engineering as a Profession," *Engineer's Week Magazine*, www.hooverassociation.org/hoover/speeches/engineering_as_a_profession.php.

[32] www.trumanlibrary.org/hoover/documents.php?page=2.

[33] NYTs obituary. October 21, 1964.

Figure 1.3 President Truman meeting with Hoover in 1945 to discuss postwar planning for Europe
Source: U.S. National Archives.

Questions to Consider

- Obviously, Hoover had difficulty changing from his engineering persona to that of a politician. In other words, he couldn't make the transition from introvert to ambivert. Hoover found out the hard way: politics is the polar opposite of engineering. Is there a place for engineers in politics?
- Elon Musk and Steve Wozniak are two examples of engineers that were able to adapt and become ambiverts when their situations required it. Why do you think Hoover couldn't duplicate their capability?
- Hoover tried to apply engineering methods to politics and the economy and failed. Are there other areas, besides politics, that the engineering mindset may have difficulty achieving success? What other areas in life where logic and reason don't play the major role?
- As of the writing of this book, we've endured almost three years of a major pandemic where emotions, extreme partisanship, and misinformation were rampant. How would Hoover had handled it? Would Hoover's engineering methods have worked better during this crisis?

CHAPTER 2

Communication

"That's one small step for man, one giant leap for mankind." This is perhaps one of the most famous phrases ever uttered by modern man. Everyone knows these were the first words spoken by Neil Armstrong as he set foot on the moon. But take a closer look, his immortal phrase really doesn't make much sense unless you add a missing *a* before *man*.

Neil Armstrong was a brilliant engineer, a graduate from Purdue, and being a seasoned fighter and test pilot, he had nerves of steel. In many ways, he represented the typical engineer, quiet, focused, hardworking, and serious. There's been a lot of controversy about what Neil Armstrong meant when he said those famous words. At one time, Armstrong claimed and some people speculate that he did pronounce *a* before *man*, but it was imperceptible because of the audio quality link from the moon. Later, the most famous astronaut admitted, he may have fluffed the most important words uttered by *a* man.

Certainly, anybody about to step onto the surface of the moon for the first time might be excused for miscommunicating a few lines. This was an intensely complicated mission costing billions of dollars that was going to accomplish President Kennedy's Cold War challenge to beat the Soviet Union to the Moon. My guess is that Neil Armstrong was the typical engineer and totally focused on getting the job done right and didn't spend too much time worrying about what he was going to say. Afterall, he had over half a billion people watching back on Earth, and he had a lot on his mind. In this case, I think in all sincerity we can excuse Neal Armstrong for a bit of miscommunication.

Neil Armstrong understood his primary goal in life was to be the best pilot he could be, and that his personality was, by nature, a bit taciturn. Several years after accomplishing his historic moon walk, he was invited to the White House to give an address. He opened his remarks by poking fun at himself saying, "Wilbur Wright once noted that the only bird that can talk was the parrot … and he didn't fly very well. So, I'll be brief."

Communication skills continue to be the number one deficiency in not only new engineering grads, but also in seasoned veterans. Engineers prefer numbers and always seem to be a somewhat less comfortable with words—both written and spoken.

But communication skills are critical for any engineer. Without the ability to clearly and concisely express yourself, you're not going to be able to convince your team, or your management, regardless of how good your design might be or how much more practical your ideas may be. "Engineers need to remember that precision with words is just as important as precision with numbers."[1]

No one is going to expect (or even want) you to write like Shakespeare, but you do need to know how to write professionally. The best way is to write as directly and as simply as possible. Regardless of the length of the paper, e-mail, or memo you are writing, you need to structure it properly. For example:

1. Your first paragraph requires a thesis statement—you need to tell your audience what you're going to do. This is the *what* portion of your paper. The thesis statement is usually the first or second sentence of your opening paragraph. "Due to its poor machineability, SA-302 Grade B carbon steel may not be appropriate for the design of this flange. I recommend the team go back and explore different grade alloys that still meet the design requirements."

2. Next, you need to clearly and logically develop your argument in the following paragraphs. You need to document your thesis statement. "SA-302 Grade B carbon steel contains high amounts of manganese and molybdenum which causes the metal to adhere to drills and cutting tools thus causing them to fracture." "Because of the large numbers of small diameter holes required, we run the risk

---

[1] A quote I never forgot from the late Professor Clive Dym of the Harvey Mudd College of Engineering during our Fifth-Year meeting at the Astronaut Beach House.

of breaking numerous drill bits which would require a large number of man hours to repair."

3. You then continue your argument, but be cognizant of the tone you are relaying to your readers. Your audience is fellow engineers, so you need to write as if you are explaining your idea or proposal to people who are familiar with the material. You respect their engineering credentials, yet you are the expert on this idea or concept you are attempting to sell. "This particular grade of steel is used primarily in pressure vessels that require a tensile strength of greater than 85ksi, which in my calculations is far more than required for this particular flange." Continue, "Because SA-302 Grade B carbon steel is primarily used for boilers and other products requiring high tensile strength, it is not a common steel and has to be special ordered, thus increasing the lead time required when ordering. Because if it's limited availability, this alloy is significantly more expensive than other steels that could be used for this application."

4. End your paper with a summary—refresh your readers with just enough information that they understand your point of view. "This grade of steel is overkill for the application we are designing, and it will increase the costs of our product significantly due to the low availability of SA 302 and its higher cost per pound than other steels. Cost for this product will also be affected by increased expense in trying to machine such a difficult alloy."

5. Show a skill in using words effectively but don't overdo it, or you'll end up sounding condescending. Use a thesaurus, but use common words that everyone understands. And look up the word in a dictionary to make sure the word you select means exactly what you want it to mean.

6. Finally, avoid using pronouns as much as possible. Pronouns are words that take the place of nouns, such as: *this, that, he, she, it, these, those,* and so on. It's better to keep using the noun throughout your paper so as not to confuse your reader. For example, in our discussion of *SA-302 Grade B carbon steel*, we continued to use that entire group of nouns or a variation such as *SA-302* or *alloy*, rather than referring to the steel as *it* or *that*.

When writing, just as in engineering design, remember the German architect, Heinrich Tessenow, who once said, "The simplest is not always the best but the best is always the simplest." Don't get fancy, keep your message brief, to the point, and simple. Your audience, whether it's a group listening to your presentation or a manager reading your e-mail, are busy professionals, and they're more interested in a direct, concise, factual explanation than a long dissertation or an overly ornate style.

Think about your writing in the same way you think about design—the best designs are simple, efficient, and robust. Just as you wouldn't design a car with an extra fifth wheel, avoid superfluous wording and take your time to select the perfect words to express your meaning. Consider good communication skills as a measure of your engineering craftsmanship.

Also, avoid emotions. As soon as you interject your personal feelings, the reader becomes circumspect of your motives. If your communication involves recommending a choice, lay out the facts in an objective way so that the reader logically comes to the same conclusion as you.

And then there's speechmaking and giving presentations to a large group of colleagues, perhaps the most difficult form of communication for anyone, engineers or not. As they say, "At a funeral, most people would rather be in the casket than giving the eulogy."

Here are some pointers when public speaking or giving presentations:

- Be prepared. Know your charts and be very familiar with your data. There's a real good chance you'll stumble if you look up at one of your slides and suddenly realize you don't recognize your own material. Never try giving a presentation with somebody else's charts.
- This is tricky, but don't overprepare to the extent that you're simply rehearsing memorized lines or you've practiced so many times you actually begin to sound bored with your own material.
- You're going to be nervous, but let that nervousness work for you, use it to energize yourself. Some people find it helpful to find an unoccupied room beforehand and just let their emotions and pre-jitters out by yelling or just psyching

themselves out by waving their arms, jumping, doing jumping jacks, and so on.

- When you start out, share something about yourself. Your audience is interested in getting to know you and will have a more favorable view of you throughout your presentation if they feel a sense that they got to know a little bit about you.

- If you're trying to get a point across or are trying to sell an idea, try telling a story. People always remember a good story that hits home a point.

- Until you're very practiced and have lots of experience giving presentations, avoid humor. Your audience isn't expecting it, and regardless of how humorous it might be, your joke may get little response, leaving you feeling awkward and embarrassed.

- Your audience is not there to criticize you or to see you fail. They want you to be successful. They would be just as disappointed to see you flounder as you would. They are on your side.

- Look at your audience but don't feel intimidated by the looks on their faces. Some may appear puzzled or skeptical, and some may even look bored. These are the same expressions people have on their faces when they're trying to hear and understand a presentation. Take it as a good sign—they're listening.

- Gesture. For some reason, when speaking in front of a group, your hands and arms suddenly feel as if they're in the way, you just don't know what to do with them. Cross them behind your back? Hold them in front? Cross them over your chest? Use them, let them help you make a connection with your words to your audience and gesture when making a point.

- You are not going to be perfect, no one is, so don't let that get you down. Even after years of giving speeches or presentations, you'll still find yourself thinking you could have done better. In most cases, you will be much harsher on yourself than your audience.

- Always know your audience. In this case, most of your presentations will be before engineers, and technical people always feel more comfortable with numbers. If your slides have numerical data, understand them thoroughly and be ready to explain them because engineers always study numbers. God forbid if your numbers don't add up.
- Finish strong. Your ending is your most critical part of your speech. This is where you sum up what you want your audience to take away from your presentation.

Whether writing or presenting, say what you need to say as concisely as possible. Remember, your audience consists of very busy people who are constrained by time. The greatest speech in American history was only 10 sentences long and was delivered in about 2 minute's time, but it will last forever. Abraham Lincoln took his time to make sure every word of his Gettysburg Address served a purpose and resonated with his audience.

There are numerous traditional ways we communicate: casual small talk, speaking engagements, written reports, presentations, e-mails, text messaging, and even our body language. Misunderstandings brought upon by poor communications make up the majority of both personal and professional mistakes you will encounter. Whether it be an e-mail with a poor selection of words or perhaps even an unintended facial expression or tone of voice interpreted by the listener as disinterest or ridicule, recall what the poet Maya Angelou once said: "People will forget what you said, people will forget what you did, but people will never forget how you made them feel."

One final suggestion concerning electronic communications: always respond, even if it just to acknowledge receipt of the e-mail or text. There are few things as unnerving as taking the time to compose an e-mail and then sit and wait as it goes unanswered. Did the recipient get it? Did he/she disagree with something you wrote? Perhaps they don't even care what you wrote? When someone takes the time to contact you, always reply or, at least respond with, a *Got it, Thanks,* or *Will respond, later.* I once had the very good fortune of reporting to one of the busiest managers within NASA, the chief engineer. Despite his workload and stress level, he always immediately responded to my e-mails. Maybe it was just a *Thank you!* or *Great* or *Let's discuss, later*, but it was reassuring that my boss considered me important enough to recognize my correspondence, and it also eliminated any mystery whether he was displeased or uninterested in what I had to say.

Suggested Resources

Kohut, M. and J. Neffinger. 2013. "Compelling People: The Hidden Qualities That Make Us Influential." Plume.

Patterson, K., J. Grenny, R. McMillan, and A. Switzler. 2011. "Crucial Conversations." McGraw Hill.

Tannen, D. 2008. "Communication Matters—He Said/She Said: Women, Men and Language." The Modern Scholar.

Van Edwards, V. 2016. "The Power of Body Language." The Great Courses.

Weber, C. 2013. "Conversational Capacity—The Secret to Building Successful Teams That Perform When the Pressure Is On." McGraw Hill.

Case Study: Fire at Mann Gulch

In July of 1805, the Lewis and Clark expedition camped for several days along the Missouri River, in what is now the state of Montana, and enjoyed the intense beauty of this remote area on their way to find the Pacific coast of North America. Meriwether Lewis described the area in his diary as "…the most remarkable clifts that we have yet seen. These clifts rise from the water's edge on either side perpendicularly to a height of 1,200 feet."[2] The explorers named the area *Gates of the Mountains* because it formed such an abrupt transition from the American Great Plains to the Rocky Mountains. Their campsite has since been called Meriwether Canyon, and directly north of it is an area called Mann Gulch.

A gulch is a steep valley carved from centuries of erosion, usually from flash floods. It is deeper than a gulley but not as deep as a canyon. At its bottom, it may contain a small stream or a dry bed. Mann Gulch is located about 30 miles directly north of Helena. There are no roads leading to Mann Gulch, and it can only be accessed first by boat along the Missouri River, and then by foot along its steep rocky slope filled with trees, tall grasses, and spring flowers.

During summer months, this pristine and beautiful area draws tourists and fishermen; in the fall, the hunters pass through in search of moose,

Figure 2.1 Mann Gulch, today. Notice the steepness of the valley sides

Source: Rodney Benson.

---

[2] *The Journals of the Lewis and Clark Expedition*, Volume 4. July 19, 1805.

black bear, deer, and mountain goat. The only year-round inhabitants are the loggers who harvest the vast and rich forests of Douglas fir and ponderosa pine nestled among juniper trees.

Such dense woodlands need to be protected from the summer lightning storms continually moving in from the eastern Great Plains. In order to help preserve these natural wonders, in 1905 President Theodore Roosevelt established the U.S. Forestry Service (USFS).

To access such remote areas as Mann Gulch, in 1940, the USFS began a new quick-strike force program called the Smokejumpers—a group of highly trained firefighters who could be dropped from a plane into isolated areas to fight the fires. The Smokejumpers were an elite group of individuals who had to be part daredevil, skilled in fighting fires, and extremely well-conditioned to jump from a C-47 into a forest fire. Knowing this was a rugged and hazardous way to make a living, the USFS had a mandatory retirement age of 40 years old and would not provide life insurance. The Smokejumpers had to rely on each other's skill and competence in such a dangerous job and developed a close bond of camaraderie when fighting fires or fighting saloon patrons in the local bars. Within the USFS, the Smokejumpers were known as an elite group of fighters, their version of the Navy's Marine Corps.

To fight fires, the Smokejumpers did not have access to water, so their tools and their methods were the most basic. They carried a shovel and a Pulaski, a long-handled tool having one side of its head shaped like an axe, while the other side had a hoe. Once they arrived at the fire, the team would proceed to dig and scrape a 2-ft.-wide ditch, called a *fire-line* along the perimeter of the fire, thus starving it of fuel when it reached the barren trench. Then, the men would enter the fire zone and proceed to bury any smoldering trees and bush to prevent burning embers (called *firebrands*) from sailing in the wind to another part of the forest. Their objective was to get to the fire while it was still small, before it became large. The USFS had a term, called *10 o'clock fires*, meaning that the Smokejumper team would be dropped onto the target fire area and would have it extinguished by 10 o'clock the next morning. To the elite Smokejumpers, fighting fires seemed a routine task, until August 5, 1949.

Leading the Smokejumpers was Wagner (*Wag*) Dodge, a man whose good looks and exceptional skills matched his rather swashbuckling name.

But Wag Dodge was anything but flamboyant or outgoing. At 33, he was by far the oldest member of the team and had been part of the Smoke-jumpers since 1941, a year after their inception, and had been a foreman since 1945. Wag Dodge had some of the qualities needed to lead a fire-fighting team, he had been described as calm, level-headed, disciplined, and imperturbable. But he was also a loner, extremely quiet, even being described as *taciturn as a tree*.[3] Years later, in describing her husband, Wag's wife recalled, "He said to me when we were married, 'You do your job and I'll do mine, and we'll get along just fine.'"

Wag was also thorough and meticulous and could build or repair almost anything. When his Smokejumpers were attending their required three-week training course, Wag missed it because management asked him to perform a variety of maintenance chores throughout the camp. It's doubtful Wag Dodge was disappointed at missing the group training.

Figure 2.2 Wag Dodge
Source: USDA Forest Service.

---

[3] K. Shulz. September 8, 2014. *The Story That Tore Through the Trees* (New York Magazine).

Wag's team consisted of 15 men, 13 were between the ages of 17 and 23. Although they all knew of him, they had never worked with him before, and Wag didn't know most of their names.

August 5, 1949, saw record high temperatures in Helena as the temperature hit 97°F, and this late in the summer, the forests were dry and at their highest risk from fire due to lightning strikes. When smoke was first spotted near the southern ridge of Mann Gulch where it joins Meriweather Canyon by one of the USFS lookout posts, a radio message was sent, and the Smokejumpers were dispatched from their camp in Missoula, about 100 miles from Mann Gulch.

Despite a great deal of air turbulence, the twin engine Douglas C-47 managed to safely drop the Smokejumpers near their target on top of Mann Gulch between 3:50 and 4:10 p.m. The tools were also dropped, but the parachute for the team's radio failed to open, and it was destroyed on impact. By 5:00 p.m., Dodge ordered the men to get organized and head down the gulch toward the Missouri River, they'd fight the fire in a much safer position with the river and the wind at their backs.

After walking about 400 yards down the gulch, they discovered a new fire was suddenly blocking their path to the safety of the river. Firebrands, pieces of burning wood, and embers from the main fire to their south had sailed through the air and started a new blaze on the northern slope between them and the safety of the river. At about 5:45 p.m., with the new fire only about 150 to 200 yards away, Dodge ordered his crew to turn around and head back up the gulch, which had a sharp 18 percent grade. The fire was now on both sides of the gulch and began pursuing the men to the stony ridge at its peak.

As they continued their trek up the steep sides of the gulch, the landscape was changing, and they were encountering more fields of tall prairie grass. The wind was also changing direction and increasing speed, and without the heavy trees blocking it, the fire would increase its speed through the fields of tall, yellow grass. Dodge realized they were in serious danger. He ordered his men to drop their tools and run up the gulch.

Within minutes, Dodge saw an open field of dry grass and suddenly stopped. Without saying anything and with his typical muted unflappability, he began to consider his next move. As his terrified team looked on incredulously, he pulled out a pack of matches, knelt down, and began to ignite the grass. Dodge's fire quickly burned the dead grass ahead of him, and as it moved away, he yelled to the others to follow him inside the ring of fire. His team of firefighters stared at him in disbelief as if he'd lost his mind, and finally one of them shouted, "The hell with that, I'm getting out of here!" The rest of the exhausted, confused men followed, perhaps seeking some semblance of conspicuous leadership or just an instance of groupthink during a traumatic crisis, and continued their desperate flight from the ensuing firestorm. Robert Sallee later stated that "We thought he must have gone nuts."

Now alone, as the maelstrom headed directly toward him, Dodge grabbed his canteen, soaked a handkerchief in water, held it against his mouth, and laid face-down on the still warm embers of his grass fire. As the fire approached, the powerful updrafts lifted Dodge's body off the ground moving him around the burn circle, but Dodge's ploy worked, and being deprived of any fuel, the huge fire went around the area he had scorched.

The rest of the Smokechasers desperately sought to get to the top of the ridge and to safety, but the higher they climbed, the steeper the ridge became. Although a man running uphill must fight gravity and obstructions, a fire travels fastest moving uphill where its intense heat draws the fresh air from the downhill side, pushing the relentless fire toward the fuel uphill that the fire has already preheated. It was a race no man could win.

The flames were approaching 1,800°F and were now just yards behind them. The scorching heat was causing the rocks to crack and burst, while firebrands began falling from the sky like mortar fragments burning their skin and starting new fires all around them. Amidst the intense smoke, heat, and overwhelming roar of the inferno, one firefighter tripped on the jagged, broken stones, fractured his leg and rolled, screaming, into the all-consuming flames.

The scorching flames starved the area of oxygen, and the exhausted men were suffocating as the heat charred their lung tissue. The area became covered in deep black smoke, and one by one, each of the exhausted, blinded men began to trip and then fall as the relentless flames finally captured its prey. The intense fire torched each body where it lay, and within seconds, burned every stitch of clothing, shoes, and adornment the men wore and sent bits of cloth, buttons, belt buckles, pieces of shoe leather, cigarettes, pocketknives, and watches billowing high into the sky. The next day a wristwatch was found with the hands melted at 5:54 p.m., where time had stood still at that moment for the pitiable man wearing it.

Only two of Dodge's men made it to the precipice and finding a crevice in the rock slid under it to the other side of the ridge, to safety. Walter Rumsey, age 21, and Robert Sallee, age 17, were desperately clinging to the rocks, and as the flames approached, Rumsey later said, "We were half hysterical."

Not far below, Wag Dodge dusted himself off and emerged from the smoke and smoldering flames and headed across the scorched landscape looking for his team. He heard someone calling for help about 200 yards away. When Dodge found the man, he was very badly burned, yet, oddly, seemed almost euphoric. He was so badly burned that his nerve endings had all been incinerated and, at the moment, was feeling no pain. Dodge carefully moved him out of the ashes and burning embers and laid him down on a long rock. Dodge decided to leave him and look for other survivors. Before he left, he considered leaving his canned potatoes for the stricken man but realized he no longer had hands with which to eat them.

After the fire had passed, Rumsey and Sallee heard a man calling for help. They found Bill Hellman just a few yards from the safety of their rock crevice. Hellman's pants and shoes had been burned off him, and large portions of flesh were hanging from his bones. He mumbled something about his wife, but in the confusion and terror, they never could hear exactly what he said.

Then they heard another voice, it was Dodge staggering up the ridge. He told them he found another survivor, badly burned, lower down the hill. Dodge couldn't remember the man's name, but thought it started with an *S*. It was Joe Sylvia.

Hellman wasn't as fortunate as Joe Sylvia, he was in excruciating pain, and at one point, begged Dodge to hit him with an axe to end his suffering.[4] It was decided that Rumsey would be left to care for Bill Hellman, while Dodge and Sallee would head to the river to get help. Before leaving, Dodge left his can of potatoes for Hellman and Rumsey.

---

[4] Interview with Richard Wilson at 4:50, www.youtube.com/watch?v=9L9kh5 OBMs8&t=1016s.

As Dodge and Sallee stumbled into the darkness toward the Missouri River, Rumsey offered the can to Hellman. The scorched man grabbed it but desperately drank the salt water, which only increased his dire thirst. As they waited for help to arrive, Walter Rumsey realized Hellman's burned flesh was giving off a terrible odor.

Dodge and Sallee finally made it through the lingering flames and the dark down to the river and encountered a boat full of tourists who were watching the fire. By early morning, a rescue team finally reached Joe Sylvia, and as they started to administer to his wounds, he pleaded, "Please...don't look at my face, it's awful!" One of the rescuers peeled an orange and fed each individual section to him.

It took five more days and 450 firefighters to finally bring the Mann Gulch fire under control. It burned 4,500 acres, over 7 square miles.

Of the 15 jumpers,[5] only three survived: Wag Dodge, Walter Rumsey, and Robert Sallee. Both Bill Hellman and Joe Sylvia later died of their wounds at the Helena hospital. Today, on the slopes of Mann Gulch, there are 12 crosses and one Star of David marking the spots where rescuers retrieved each of the bodies.

The tragic events at Mann Gulch shocked the American public and brought a great deal of political and media scrutiny to the USFS. The Forest Service was criticized for insufficiently training the Smokejumpers and recklessly sending them to their deaths at Mann Gulch. Before long, the USFS was embroiled in a lawsuit from the distraught families of the deceased claiming negligence and contending Dodge's fire was the one that actually killed their sons and husbands.

Opponents accused the Forest Service of hiding evidence and even coercing witnesses as they were determined to fight back and protect their reputation. The Forest Service convened a Board of Review[6] that eventually exonerated the USFS by stating the Mann Gulch fire, at the time

---

[5] There was a 16th man, James Harrison, who also perished in the fire. He was not part of the Smokejumper team and had already been on the ground fighting the fire before Dodge and his team landed. He joined and perished with the Smokejumpers as they tried to escape the fire.

[6] www.nwcg.gov/sites/default/files/wfldp/docs/sr-mg-report-of-board-of-review.pdf.

of the jump, was a typical fire and that the Smokejumpers were ably led by Wag Dodge who on several occasions, including lighting his escape fire, made correct decisions. They partly based their findings on signed testimony, including that of the 17-year-old survivor, Robert Sallee, who stated that the entire team would have been saved had they followed Dodge into the escape fire and the escape fire was not responsible for the others' deaths.

But, as a result of the Board of Review, the USFS also vastly overhauled its training and later developed and incorporated the *Ten Standard Firefighting Orders*[7] into firefighter training. The USFS also began a comprehensive study of the science of fires and instituted new fire laboratories to help understand the characteristics of forest fires. Much later, the Mann Gulch tragedy also caused the USFS to reconsider risking lives to fight forest fires as a new viewpoint emerged that lightning strikes and forest fires are more of a natural occurrence that in the long run creates healthier and more resilient forests.

There has always been the lingering question: How, while in the midst of the most infernal danger, and with only seconds to think, did Wag Dodge suddenly *invent* his escape fire?[8] Where did this stroke of innovative thinking come from? The Board of Review also wanted to know and inquired if he had ever heard of such a technique before or had anyone ever trained him how to make one. Dodge simply responded in his reticent way, "Not that I know of. It just seemed the logical thing to do."

Whether it was Dodge's original order to head down the gulch to fight the fire, or head back and drop all their tools, or his escape fire, survivor Rumsey later told the investigation board that "Dodge had a characteristic in him. It's hard to tell what he is thinking."

The tragedy at Mann Gulch made it into popular culture in 1952 with the release of *Red Skies of Montana,* starring Richard Widmark in a role loosely based on Wag Dodge, and again in 2004, when Canadian folksong singer/writer, James Keelaghan, composed, *Cold Missouri Waters,*

---

[7] www.nwcg.gov/committee/6mfs/10-standard-firefighting-orders.

[8] Although there is some evidence American Indians had used this technique to save themselves from grass fires, Wag Dodge may unknowingly have re-invented a technique that is still used today.

a somber ballad where a dying Wag Dodge reflects on the fire from his hospital bed but says he has nothing to confess.

The tragedy at Mann Gulch has been written about profusely and used in a variety of training programs. In 1992, Norman Maclean published *Young Men and Fire*, using both Walter Rumsey and Robert Sallee as sources. Maclean's book won the National Book Critics Circle Award in 1992.

Walter Rumsey and Robert Sallee made a few more jumps together before leaving the USFS. They had kept in touch and even visited Mann Gulch together in 1978. But in 1980, finally, nature's wrath, combined with human error, once again caught up with Walter Rumsey. He was traveling on a business trip for the U.S. Soil Conservation Service when his commuter plane encountered tremendous thunderstorms, causing both engines to stall, crashing in a Nebraska field. The crash report stated: "Engine failure due to massive ingestion of water into both engines. Crew error. Unwise decision to enter area of thunderstorms."[9] Walter Rumsey died at age of 52.

Robert Sallee, the last survivor of the Mann Gulch fire, died in 2014 at the age of 82. He stayed on with the USFS for a while and made four more jumps before deciding to go back to school. He earned an accounting degree and had a successful career at the Inland Empire Paper Company.

His son said, he rarely spoke about Mann Gulch. "I think there were two reasons for that" Eric Sallee said in an interview. "First, he was 17, and he'd had an absolutely traumatic experience. He helped haul those bodies off the mountain the next day." And second, Robert Sallee still felt the special camaraderie for his deceased friends whose skill and faith in each other could mean life or death. He knew the families of those men were infuriated with the USFS and, "They thought the escape fire killed their kids, and my dad had to testify in court proceedings. The whole thing was a nasty experience."

Some folks claimed the seemingly imperturbable Wag Dodge never recovered from the tragedy at Mann Gulch. After the fire, his once

---

[9] R. Kebabjian. n.d. "1980 Accident Details," www.usdeadlyevents.com/1980-june -12-air-wisconsin-flight-965-crash-storm-engine-failure-valley-ne-13/.

Figure 2.3 Robert Sallee (left) and Walter Rumsey
Source: USDA Forest Service.

skillful and industrious hands began to constantly shake. But they were mistaken, and they underestimated Wag Dodge. He had contracted Parkinson's disease and died six years after his nightmare at Mann Gulch in January 1955.

Years afterward, asked by a reporter to describe her deceased husband, Dodge's widow Patsy, said: "I loved him very much, but I didn't know him very well."

Questions to Consider

- Robert Sallee said afterward that he believed all 15 men could have been saved had they followed Wag Dodge into his *escape fire*. His crew knew he had impeccable reputation as a fire fighter; why didn't they follow him?
- The most skilled men and women are often promoted to management. Does this sometimes mean an organization

loses these skills, while at the same time, gaining a poor leader? What other types of skills does someone need when they move into a management/leadership role?

- Wag Dodge, under life and death pressure with only minutes to live, displayed an incredible ability to innovate on the spot by creating the *escape fire*. True innovation often means discovering something completely opposite to what you've believed or how you've been trained. Starting a fire to fight a fire is obviously a concept that would be difficult to accept, especially under these circumstances. Could Wag Dodge have done anything different to convince his team to follow him into the escape fire?

Case Study: A Failure to Communicate Between Project Office and Prime Contractor

NASA Discovers a Hostile New World

During the Apollo program, NASA had been viewed as a shining example of American technology, innovation, and organizational expertise, but two decades after the moon landings, NASA saw its sterling reputation begin to tarnish.

After the sixth and final moon landing by Apollo 17 in December of 1972, the American public lost interest in the space program. What was previously seen as one of the most important human feats in history was now viewed as common place and costly. American politicians and voters began doubting the need for an expensive space program while the nation was involved in the Vietnam War, continuing social unrest while enduring an inflationary economy.

After years of debate, NASA was finally given the funding to develop the Space Transportation System (STS), better known as the Space Shuttle Program. It was sold to Congress as a reusable spacecraft that could be launched once a week and dramatically bring down the cost of access to space. The first shuttle launched in April of 1981 and, although a technical achievement, the shuttle never came close to living up to the promises made to Congress and the American people. The program could only average four to five flights per year, and with a cost per launch approaching half a billion dollars, launching hardware to space aboard the shuttle was almost four times as costly as an expendable launch vehicle. It was also plagued by countless launch delays due to technical problems and weather.

In 1986, NASA's situation grew much worse as the Rodgers Commission, appointed by President Reagan, investigated the Shuttle Challenger's catastrophic explosion, resulting in the tragic loss of seven astronauts. The commission blamed NASA's culture and bludgeoned agency management in its final report.

Things didn't get better for the space agency through the next decade. In 1990, the 12-billion-dollar Hubble Telescope, after numerous delays, was finally launched when astronomers soon discovered their much-vaunted telescope was nearsighted and unusable due to a simple manufacturing error. Before long, NASA found itself in an unaccustomed spot—the butt of late-night jokes. The very popular *Late Show with David Letterman* offered up a *Top Ten List of Hubble Telescope Excuses*, including such quips as, "Some kids on Earth must be fooling around with a garage door opener." As well as "There's a doohickey rubbing against the part that looks kind of like a cowboy hat."[10]

The next year, 1991, the antennae of the 600-million-dollar Gamma Ray Observatory failed to deploy when it became entangled in a thermal blanket. Shuttle astronauts had to perform an unplanned spacewalk to unjam the antennae, saving the scientific probe. Later that week, Letterman presented, "Top Ten Ways Our Lives Will Be Better Now That They Fixed That Satellite," with number six being, "NASA employees no longer have to lie about where they work."[11]

By this time, the agency found itself in the uncomfortable position of trying to justify and find a use for its fleet of space shuttles by proposing an orbiting space station. An agency that once always got its way with Congress was now facing serious threats of cutbacks and even closures to some of its research centers. The space station proposal passed, albeit much reduced in scope, by a single vote. Not the type of support NASA was used to during its Apollo days. Afterward, President Clinton promised dubious voters that changes were in order and stated "We are going to redesign NASA at the same time we redesign the space station."

NASA's Situation Gets Worse: The Mars Surveyor 1998 Program and a Failure to Communicate

The Mars Surveyor 1998 Program was going to be NASA's return to the red planet after almost 20 years since the successful Viking Missions of the mid-1970s. Mars Surveyor consisted of two spacecraft, the Mars Climate Orbiter, which would launch first and insert itself in an orbit of the planet, while the Mars Polar Lander would launch a year later and touch down on the Martian surface.

---

[10] Late Show with David Letterman. September 6, 1993.
[11] Late Show with David Letterman. May 5, 1992.

On December 11, 1998, NASA launched the Jet Propulsion Laboratory's (JPL), Mars Climate Orbiter onboard a Delta II rocket from the Cape Canaveral Air Station, Florida. This 193-million-dollar probe was designed to enter Martian orbit and study weather and climate conditions on the planet for one year and then act as a communications relay for NASA's Mars Polar Lander that was to land three months later on the southern pole of Mars to study the planet's water and carbon dioxide levels as well as climate history.

During the Mars Climate Orbiter's nine-month journey, the number of extra commands the spacecraft's computer was making to the thrusters to maneuver its trajectory toward Mars puzzled flight controllers. The number of course correction firings didn't match their calculations.

In September of 1999, 286 days after launch, the Climate Orbiter began its insertion maneuver to enter the Martian orbit. The probe went into a communication blackout as it entered the far side of Mars 49 seconds earlier than flight controllers at NASA's Jet Propulsion Lab had anticipated. The controllers never regained contact.

Afterward, investigators discovered that the software written by the prime contractor, Lockheed Martin, had been using English units, whereas the JPL team had been using metric units, as specified in the original contract with Lockheed Martin. When controllers called for the burn, they were assuming forces in metric units of Newton, whereas the software was telling the probe in English units of Pound-force. The unexpected flight corrections made throughout the flight, conducted in Pounds-force rather than in Newtons, caused the Climate Orbiter to be almost 170 kilometers (106 miles) lower in the Martian atmosphere than expected. One pound-force is equal to 4.448 Newtons.

The probe most likely burned up in the Martian atmosphere or, possibly, bounced off it into an unknown journey through the solar system.

In January of 1999, while the Mars Climate Orbiter was still eight months from arriving at Mars, NASA followed with the 110-million-dollar Mars Polar Lander, which reached Mars orbit in December of 1999. But as it entered the Martian atmosphere, its computer software misinterpreted vibrations coming from a sensor on its landing legs as an actual touchdown on the surface and then shut off its descent engine.

No longer in a controlled descent, the probe violently crashed into the red planet's surface, resulting in another complete loss of mission.

Later that week, Letterman read, "Top Ten Signs Your New Job Isn't Working Out" with Number 6 being, "You work for NASA and your title is 'executive in charge of space probe quality control.'"[12]

Late night viewers (such as this NASA employee) couldn't find much relief from the ridicule. Turning the channel to the NBC affiliate, Jay Leno joked, "According to a disturbing new report, math scores are down 20% and reading scores are down 30%. Science scores are down a whopping 50%, and that's just at NASA headquarters!" Continuing, "We kid NASA, but it hasn't had a good track record in the past few months. In September we lost the Mars Observer. Then we lost the Mars Polar Lander. In fact, today Mars concluded that there is no intelligent life on Earth!"[13]

In retrospect, a lot of the problems NASA encountered in the 1980s and 1990s were later seen as a result of the agency implementing a *faster, better, cheaper* approach to flight hardware. At the time, NASA management was determined to stifle political and the public concerns over the cost of a space program.

It took decades, along with a string of sensational technical successes, for NASA to rebuild its reputation with the American public. As NASA moved on from *better, faster, cheaper*, it was able to produce such stunning engineering accomplishments as the Hubble repair mission, the International Space Station, the Kepler Mission and the discovery of exoplanets, the Cassini Mission to Saturn, Juno's rendezvous with Jupiter, New Horizon's flyby of Pluto, and a renaissance at the Jet Propulsion Lab, an organization that learned from its mistakes, and conquered the complexities of exploring the Red Planet by landing five rovers,[14] two of which are still patrolling the Martian surface.

---

[12] September 1, 1993.

[13] www.latimes.com/archives/la-xpm-1999-dec-15-cl-43969-story.html.

[14] List of Mars Exploration Rovers (MER): *Sojourner* (1997), *Opportunity* (2002), *Spirit* (2003), *Curiosity* (2011), and *Perseverance* (2020). *Curiosity* and *Perseverance* are still active.

In 2005, researchers using the Mars Global Surveyor that has been orbiting and mapping the planet since 1997 believe they spotted the crash site and debris field of the Mars Polar Lander.[15]

Questions to Consider

- NASA supporters and enthusiasts have always defended failures by reminding sceptics that "Space is hard." But these failures all had root causes in very simple reasons where, objectively, it is hard to defend. NASA and its contractors got all the *hard* stuff right; it was the easy stuff they got wrong. In your experience, how often do you concentrate on getting the difficult parts right while ignoring the simple parts?

- The Mars Climate Orbiter was lost because of a communications failure between contractors and NASA. It takes years to design and develop a space craft. How is it conceivable that throughout the design and manufacturing process, as well as when controllers found themselves puzzled by the probe's correction burns, contractors at Lockheed Martin and officials at JPL didn't have a simple discussion or briefing that would have easily clarified and solved such a miscommunication? In your experience, have you ever just assumed the other party must know or be aware of a fact you consider simple?

- Comedians David Letterman and Jay Leno may not possess the technical expertise to design highly complicated spacecraft, but they do have the ability, and the right, to communicate the embarrassing problems NASA encountered to a huge audience of viewers. Is it the little things (such as simple communication) that count? If the Mars Climate Orbiter and Polar Lander had failed due to a much more complex reason such as radiation damage to electrical components or damage from micro meteors, would the comedians and the public have been more forgiving?

---

[15] www.space.com/1153-mars-polar-lander-clues-crash-site.html.

Case Study: Did Lee's Inability to Communicate Save the Union at Gettysburg?

For every Southern boy fourteen years old, not once but whenever he wants it, there is the instant when it's still not yet two o'clock on that July afternoon in 1863...[16]

In April of 1861, newly elected president, Abraham Lincoln, was facing civil war. South Carolina had fired the opening shots at the federal base at Fort Sumter and seven southern states had already seceded from the union.

Lincoln suddenly needed a warrior to lead the federal troops of the north against the southern rebellion. The obvious man he wanted was Robert E. Lee.

Lee had an impeccable resume being the son of a revolutionary war hero and was related by marriage to the Father of the Country, George Washington. He had finished second in his class at West Point and, in a record still held today, graduated without receiving a single demerit. Lee went on to military successes throughout the Mexican War and returned to Washington D.C. and the War Department where Winfield Scott, the Commanding General of the U.S. Army and who had served under seven presidents, became his mentor and trusted friend.

After the first shots were fired at Fort Sumter, Lee's home state of Virginia voted to withdraw from the union. Lincoln offered Lee a Major General's position to lead Union forces against the rebellion, but Lee declined and resigned his commission in the U.S. Army, telling Scott he could never draw a sword against his fellow Virginians. General Winfield Scott replied, "You have made the greatest mistake of your life."

In America, during the 19th century Lee, as many people, both north and south, considered themselves first as a citizen of their home state and second as an American. After all, Virginia had been a commonwealth for 254 years, while the fledging United States had only been a nation for 73 years.

---

[16] W. Faulkner. n.d. *Intruder in the Dust.*

Lee was appointed by the Confederate president, Jefferson Davis, in 1862, to lead the Army of Northern Virginia (ANV) against the Union's Army of the Potomac. After a string of battlefield victories along the Virginia peninsula, at the Second Battle of Bull Run, Fredericksburg, and Chancellorsville, the North found itself in a desperate situation. After the union's loss at Fredericksburg, Lincoln told a colleague, "If there's a place worse than hell, I'm in it."

In reality, Lee's and the South's position wasn't much better. Lee's victories may have kept the southern capital, Richmond, safe from the Army of the Potomac, but the countless battles and skirmishes and two huge foraging armies had destroyed much of Lee's beloved Virginia.

After so many battles, Lee had developed a special working relationship with many of his generals such as Stonewall Jackson, whom he called his *right arm*, the flamboyant calvary general J.E.B. Stuart, with his youthful gait and festooned hat, captured southern imagination with his gallant rides, and James Longstreet, who Lee referred to as his *old warhorse*.

Lee and the South took another blow when Stonewall Jackson was killed during the Battle of Chancellorsville. With the death of Stonewall, Lee undertook the massive and complicated procedure of reorganizing the command structure within the ANV, bringing in numerous new less experienced officers into the army. This would prove problematic for Lee and his new officer corps.

Lee was a brilliant leader, and his style of issuing *discretionary orders* to his officers on the field he was certainly ahead of his times. Lee developed a deep trust in his officers and delegated to them the authority to make tactical decisions in the field because they were closest to the action. Lee's generals enjoyed his trust and enjoyed the flexibility allowed to them by *discretionary orders*. But in order for subordinates to work for a unified goal and not just do what they want, it is critical they understand their commander's *intent*; that is the overall objective of a military campaign.

When Lee began his march into Pennsylvania, there was already significant confusion about his intent. Most of Lee's correspondence at the time clearly stated he wished to remain in the north for as long as possible to relieve the effects of war on the South. President Davis, as well as General Longstreet, were under the impression the move was to relocate the battlefield to the North in order to relieve the southern farmers while the very presence of an enemy army on their soil would terrify and influence an already demoralized northern population as Lincoln's re-election approached. The invasion date was set to mid-summer to allow the ANV to forage and live off the countless acres of northern farms. Most importantly, Longstreet believed he had an agreement with Lee to avoid any major battles with the northern army. If forced to fight, they were to move into defensive positions and inflict as many causalities to the North while avoiding any major losses to their already depleted forces.

Such a major operation required cavalry support. Lee relied on General J. E. B. Stuart to not only move ahead of his lumbering foot soldiers to provide reconnaissance and reports of the enemy location but also to protect the ANV's flank as they moved through enemy territory.

Although Lee reminded Stuart that he was the *eyes and ears* of the army, he also gave him wide discretionary orders. Stuart, always looking for a chance to enhance his reputation on the pages of southern newspapers, may have sent his cavalry northward in search of glory rather than undertake the less ostentatious task of scouting for enemy movements. Stuart actually lost track of Lee and the Army of Northern Virginia, which was now blindly moving through enemy territory, and on July 1, 1863, it found itself near a small town in the Pennsylvania countryside named Gettysburg. Lee discovered the Union's Army of the Potomac's location before his cavalry general and found his enemy entrenched on higher ground.

Although faced with an army larger than his own and over 100 miles deep into enemy territory, Lee seems to have changed his mind about avoiding large engagements with his northern adversary. Lee was very confident in the Army of Northern Virginia. These ragged, often starving young men had continually defeated and sent much better equipped and supplied Union soldiers running for their lives. Some historians have described the Army of Northern Virginia as one of the greatest fighting forces of all time. Such victories often give infantry soldiers a sense of confidence and a psychological advantage over their enemy, but it also can give a commanding general a false sense of bravado. Lee decided to change tactics, that is, his intent, and destroy the Union army.

On the first day of battle, it appeared once again as if Lee might be on the verge of another major victory. Astride his horse, he viewed General

Ewell's 2nd Corp push Northern forces out of the town where they began to gather and reform their lines atop Cemetery Hill. Lee dispatched a messenger with the order, "Take the hill, if practicable, but don't bring on a general engagement." Richard Ewell had been a corps commander for only a month. He was confused at this critical moment of the battle and wasn't sure what his commanding officer meant. He had no reconnaissance and had no idea what kind of strength the Union had on Cemetery Hill. If he attacked, would he be disobeying orders and "bring on a general engagement"? As Day one of Gettysburg came to a close, Ewell decided to stop his pursuit. The weakened, demoralized Union forces on Cemetery Hill were allowed to fight another day.

On the morning of July 2, General Longstreet met with General Lee and was exasperated after hearing Lee's change of intent to engage the Union army. Longstreet argued against taking the offensive. Lee was determined and said, "If the enemy is there tomorrow, I will attack him." Longstreet replied, "If he is there tomorrow it is because he wants you to attack."

Late that evening, Lee informed Longstreet and his staff to prepare for a major attack the next morning. Lee decided to gamble and assault the Union forces where they least expect it—directly at the center of their line. He believed his army, which has always won for him in the past, can brave one last great battle that will finally crush the North. He informed a stunned and despondent Longstreet to order General George Pickett to prepare his 15,000 men to charge up Cemetery Ridge the next afternoon…

Five months later, President Lincoln visited Gettysburg to dedicate a new national cemetery. Because all previous battles had been held on southern lands where the Union was forced to retreat, this was the first time during the long, bloody war that the North could actually bury their dead in with dignity in national cemetery. As he rose to speak, the president delivered what has become known as *The Gettysburg Address.* Abraham Lincoln was able to communicate the horrors of war as well as the promise of freedom in a mere 272 words.

…that we here highly resolve that these dead shall not have died in vain—that this nation, under God, shall have a new birth of

freedom—and that government of the people, by the people, for the people, shall not perish from the earth.

Questions to Consider

- Lee's style of issuing *discretionary orders* to his commanders was innovative for the times and certainly proved successful up until the Battle of Gettysburg. Today, it is ordinary practice in the U.S. military: "One of the essential elements of a successful military campaign is the ability of the commander to precisely define his intent and communicate that intent to his key subordinates."[17] Communication skills involve the ability to clearly state one's intent.

- One the late afternoon of the first day of battle, Lee told General Ewell to take Cemetery Hill *if practicable*. Lee and Stonewall Jackson developed an extraordinary ability to understand each other's intent. Historian James M. McPherson once wrote, "Had (Stonewall) Jackson still lived, he undoubtedly would have found it practicable. But Ewell was not Jackson."[18] Ewell may not have been Stonewall Jackson, but is it his fault, or Lee's fault that Cemetery Hill wasn't taken on the late afternoon of the first day of battle?

---

[17] CDR S.S. Funk. May 1993. *The Gettysburg Campaign—Lee's Failure to Define Intent* (Naval War College).

[18] J.M. MacPherson. n.d. *Battle Cry of Freedom, the Civil War Era*, p. 654.

CHAPTER 3

Critical Thinking Skills

When Abraham Lincoln first took office, he was under enormous pressure from the Radical Republicans to simply free all the slaves and immediately grant them citizenship, including voting rights. During a meeting at the White House, the firebrand senator from Massachusetts, Charles Sumner, the leader of the Radical Republicans, called the new president weak and cowardly, and berated him, telling Lincoln he was afraid to do what was right and just.

Lincoln's ultimate goal was to free the slaves, but as the southern states were seceding and threatening a civil war, the new president desperately needed to protect his flank and keep the border states of Kentucky and Maryland in the Union. If he freed the slaves and granted citizenship at this stage of the nascent conflict, Kentucky and Maryland would certainly have joined the Confederacy.

Lincoln was brilliant at reducing complex situations by telling simple stories. The president calmly responded to the angry senator by reminding him that when one is on a journey, one uses a compass to point the way. But, unfortunately, one can't always follow the exact course prescribed by the compass needle because one might encounter swamps or mountains or even dangerous Indians. It's seldom a direct route to one's destination; therefore, one needs to follow the general direction of the compass because following the direct path one may never reach their destination. Certainly, one must always know *due north* and where they want to go, but also realize getting there safely can be a round-about way.

In fact, the Radical Republicans were right, and Lincoln agreed with their premise: slavery was an evil, and it could only be solved by emancipation. But the young president, who would ultimately give his life for the cause both he and the Radical Republicans sought, understood such issues can be extremely complex, and in order to achieve one's goal, it was necessary to consider the entire context of the situation before acting.

Proper, correct thinking, like leadership and the ability to communicate, is a learned skill. Critical thinking skills and techniques were taught by the ancient Greek philosopher, Socrates, and are now described as the *Socratic method*. When approached with a new idea or a new approach, Socrates suggested asking numerous, focused questions in order to verify the logic of the idea and to determine its validity.

The basic approach to critical thinking follows Socrates' method of investigation or cross-examination and can be categorized as:

- Examine the premise and challenge the assumption:
  - Is this always the case?
  - How do you know?
  - What is the problem you are trying to solve?
- Examine logic:
  - What's the other side of the argument?
  - Where did you get your information? How reliable is it?
  - Is any data missing?
  - Have we encountered this before?
- Be aware of motivations:
  - What's in this for you? Who is going to benefit?
  - Are there ulterior motives?
- Think through implications:
  - What would the consequences be?
  - How would this affect the rest of the system?
  - What if you're wrong? What do we lose?
  - What is the best/worst-case scenario?

Critical thinking skills also require one to be aware of our own limitations and our abilities to process data. For example, sometimes we need to doubt, or at least be cognizant of our ability to process what our senses are telling us. We can't always trust our mind's ability to perceive. Magicians rely on the sleight of hand where our eyes can't detect a movement or by tricking our mind to focus on the wrong thing.

Our memory, regardless of age, too often delivers incorrect data. Accurately remembering something you saw or experienced diminishes greatly over time. Unfortunately, even as we forget the details or even the context of what may have happened, we tend to stubbornly hold on to our questionable version until proven wrong.

As humans, we can also lose our ability to think critically when we allow emotions to rule our decision-making process. This can easily be seen in such areas as politics where even the most logical person can be persuaded by his/her emotions when confronted by a charismatic personality. When one says, "the crowd was hypnotized by the speaker," in many cases, that is almost true.

Then there's the idea of intuition. Many people, "just have a feeling about something" or believe they can, *read people* or their *gut just tells them* how to make a decision. And sometimes they're right. Our brains are always looking for patterns or similarities, and it happens instantaneously without a person consciously triggering it. We're looking for cues, something that we're familiar with or dealt with previously. For example, a nurse may be with a patient but notices something just isn't right despite the patient's charts showing everything is nominal. The data says everything is fine, but the nurse *knows* something is wrong with her patient. A parent can tell when something just feels wrong about a child. The child is just acting differently, something must be bothering them despite their denials. An auto mechanic has a gut feeling that something just isn't right with the way a car engine sounds. He has heard thousands of engines idling, but this one sounds different, despite what his diagnostic information is telling him.

Intuition is real, but it is something one gains over time and with a great deal of experience.

For an engineer, there are dangers relying on intuition versus formal analysis. Intuition may be trusted as a lead or as a possibility, but it must also be proven and verified.

Understanding and recognizing cognitive biases are crucial for developing critical thinking skills. These are internal predispositions that we may already have but are unaware of them. There are numerous cognitive biases, but some of the most common and more important ones for decision making, and for engineers, in particular, are listed as follows:

- Overconfidence bias: Just as the name implies, humans tend to internally predict overly optimistic future results. We overestimate our talent or skill or overestimate a system's reliability or functionality. This bias was partially responsible when NASA managers were overconfident in the Space Shuttle's dependability and launched Challenger in freezing weather and Columbia when they knew foam strikes occurred regularly at launch.

- Anchoring bias: A person depends too much on the first piece of data they receive and uses that as the focal point in the decision-making process. Automobile manufacturers use this technique to skew your negotiations over a new car. You see the sticker price and then negotiate from there. The dealer is the only one who knows the true cost of the car, so the MSRP is almost meaningless to the buyer, it's just the dealer's starting point in a negotiation. When the buyer purchases the car under the Manufacturer's Suggested Retail Price (MSRP), they feel like they must have made a good deal.

- Availability bias: Base a decision on information that is readily available. No deep dives are done to uncover more reliable data. The classic example of an availability bias is a person who suddenly becomes afraid of flying after reading about a plane crash and insists on driving. In reality, if one digs a little deeper into the data, it will show that plane crashes are rare events, and a person is much more likely to die in a car accident than from a plane crash.

- Confirmation bias: Seek out and rely on information and data that confirm one's views: seeking *affirmation* rather than *information*. Especially today, with social media playing such a huge role in disseminating news as well as partisan news outlets, people have a tendency to only listen to news coverage that suits their own political beliefs and become unwilling to accept data that may conflict with their beliefs.

- False equivalence bias: When a person compares two very different items or issues that may share a few characteristics but attempts to define them as equal or similar. For example, comparing apples to oranges. Both are round, both are fruit, and both grow on trees; therefore, they must taste the same.

False equivalence is often seen in political discussions and called *moral equivalencies*. An example would be comparing a modern democracy that permits capital punishment to Hitler's Germany or Stalin's Soviet Union.

- Hindsight bias: Looking back at complex failure or disaster and believe it should have been easily foreseeable and prevented. Hindsight is 20/20. Hindsight bias can be troublesome because it will lead one to greatly underestimate the failure being examined, creating a condescending sense of superiority that doesn't allow one to fully take into account the total context from which the failure may have occurred.

- Illusory correlation bias: Basing one outcome on the outcome of a totally unrelated event. Seeing a cause-and-effect outcome where one does not exist. An example would be going to a movie theater and sitting near several people talking throughout the movie, then deciding you'll never go back to that theater because the audience is rude.

- Recency effect: Basing a decision on information that only involves the most recent data, ideas, arguments, or information you've received. For example, basing a decision on the information given to you by the last person you spoke, or recalling only what you heard, or read most recently and basing your decision on that information. An unfortunate example of the recency effect is when several people are being interviewed for a job. The interviewer often remembers more about the last person he/she interviewed than about the first person interviewed.

- Sunk cost effect bias: You've invested so much money, or time, or effort into an asset that you continue to utilize that asset even when it is underperforming. Have you ever purchased an expensive item, such as a new pair of shoes, but soon discover they are not as comfortable as you hoped for? You continue to wear them, rather than your older, more comfortable shoes despite your sore feet simply because you've invested so much in them.

- IKEA effect bias: This bias is obviously named after the famous Swedish furniture store and results when one puts a lot of time and effort into a certain project, they have a tendency to favor that project over others. This can be a critical issue for any engineer involved in, for example, a design review, to maintain objectivity after putting a lot of resources into a particular project.

It's pretty obvious how dangerous any of these biases could be when one is about to make a significant decision. How to guard against these cognitive biases? It's not easy because these can be well entrenched in our personality or even within our human nature. The first step is to be aware of them and constantly and honestly consider them when making a decision. Second, make team members play the devil's advocate and question everything, including your premise. Third, review previous decisions that you now considered flawed and see what cognitive biases you may have inadvertently fallen victim to. Four, seek an objective observer's input. Also, too often, people feel a need to make a quick decision that may make them appear decisive but, if the situation doesn't call for it, take your time to sincerely reflect and study the situation in order to make the right decision.

Suggested Resources

Novella, S. 2013. "Your Deceptive Mind: A Scientific Guide to Critical Thinking Skills." The Great Courses.
Roberto, M. 2013. "The Art of Critical Decision Making." The Great Courses.
Sapolsky, R. 2012. "Being Human: Life Lessons From the Frontier of Science." The Great Courses.

Case Study: Determining the Cause of Sudden Infant Death Syndrome and Its Consequences

Background and Symptoms: The Industrial Revolution

During the 19th century, as the Industrial Revolution steamrolled through Europe, and later the United States, it transformed almost every aspect of Western culture. The intellectual advances made during the Enlightenment were now focusing logic and reason on the more practical arts of agriculture, engineering, and manufacturing. No longer were everyday items individually handcrafted, but new methods of mass production were being invented and implemented. With the division of labor and the dramatic increase of productivity, scarcity suddenly turned to abundance. Products that were once considered luxuries were now quickly becoming everyday consumer goods as the newly developed, and now ubiquitous, steam engine powered the trains and ships carrying these mass-produced goods to markets around the world.

As the Industrial Revolution continued its relentless transformation of almost every aspect of 19th century society, it produced an upper class of immense wealth and a new bourgeoisie middle class alongside the intense poverty of the lower classes.

Cities were overcrowded, particularly the poor and working-class neighborhoods where the infrastructure couldn't keep up with the sewage and clean drinking water demands of a rapidly expanding urban population. Unsanitary conditions were breeding grounds for such diseases as cholera, typhoid, typhus, and smallpox.

The labor market was transformed from individual craftsmen working in local shops to legions of anonymous men, women, and even children working in giant, cavernous factories powered almost exclusively by burning coal, which caused huge clouds of dark dust to continually block out sunlight. No longer were these new city dwellers enjoying the fresh air of the countryside, but now, with every breath, they inhaled sulfur dioxide, nitrogen oxides, and particulate matter, which, without any medical support, caused a lifetime of serious respiratory, cardiovascular, as well as neurological issues.

There were no labor or safety regulations, and the average factory worker or coal miner could expect to work 12 to 16 hours a day, six days a week. Child labor was widespread throughout the Industrial Revolution, and laws regulating it weren't passed in Great Britain or the United States until well into the 1930s.

Diagnosis and Complications: The Rise of Modern Medicine

Employing this new reliance on scientific thought and technological progress spawned by this new machine age, the science of medicine changed and became more formal, empirical, and regulated. New advances in medical studies by Louis Pasteur helped develop vaccines against anthrax and rabies, Wilhelm Roentgen discovered X-rays, Gregor Mendel drew up his laws of inheritance beginning the study of genetics, Dmitri Mendeleev developed the Periodic table, and Sigmund Freud started the new field of modern psychology with the advent of his psychoanalytic theory.

The practice of medicine, as well as training medical doctors also changed. Previously, anyone could practice medicine if they were able to pay for a diploma, and most doctors concentrated on setting bones, sewing up wounds, and conducting the almost inescapable and counter-productive task of *bleeding* a patient to cure almost any ailment. In an era before germ theory, surgeries consisted mostly of extracting bullets and performing amputations, and were done without anesthesia or any concern for cleanliness. Hospitals had been places to basically house the sick and injured, keeping them isolated from the general population.

Now, prospective students, including women for the first time, were selected on merit and were required to attend formal lectures and clinical pathology labs as well as participate in a structured program that lasted several years before being awarded a degree. Moving away from the superstitions and often backward medical practices of the past, now medical schools studied treatments based on science and supported by the continual wave of innovations and products spurred by the Industrial Revolution. Medical students concentrated on preventive medicine and 19th-century hospitals evolved into care centers where patients were treated for their ailments.

With such dramatic advances, cadavers now became an essential tool used to instruct medical students in the study of pathology and anatomy, but incorrupt corpses were not easily found for dissection. The rising middle class, along with the upper classes, had a particularly distinct repugnance to bequeathing their own or offering the bodies of family members for scientific experimentation due to a variety of legal, personal, religious, or cultural convictions. Many of these attitudes persist, even today, as some people are reluctant to volunteer and sign up as organ donors on their drivers' licenses.

To compensate for the lack of cadavers, anatomy departments had to seek other, sometimes less respectable, avenues to procure dead bodies for dissection and study. Because supply could never satisfy the demand, a new rather unpalatable, yet lucrative, occupation arose called the *resurrectionist*. These macabre entrepreneurs would closely observe recent deaths within a village or town, then simply wait for a burial to end and rob the graves in the middle of the night. The resurrectionists became so prevalent that many families often laid watch over their dead to protect them from disinterment.

Treatment: "I Have Seen My Death!"

In 1895, as medical research continued its relentless advances, Wilhelm Roentgen happened upon X-rays while applying high voltage to a cathode ray tube in his laboratory at Würzburg University in Germany. Roentgen noticed that if he placed a solid item near the fluorescent green light emanating from the tube, he could see inside the object. Further experiments with his new creation included photographing his wife Anna's hand to view the bones under her skin. Terrified, Anna, the first person ever to view her own internal bones and tissue screamed, "I have seen my death!" and never again returned to her husband's laboratory to help him.

At the time, Roentgen and other researchers like the French scientist, Marie Curie, didn't understand the dangers of radiation. They considered X-rays as simply another variant of a typical light ray but obviously more intense. In reality, X-rays are another version of light but in a much more dangerous way than researchers at the time understood. The X-rays being emitted from Roentgen's cathode ray tube had much shorter wavelengths

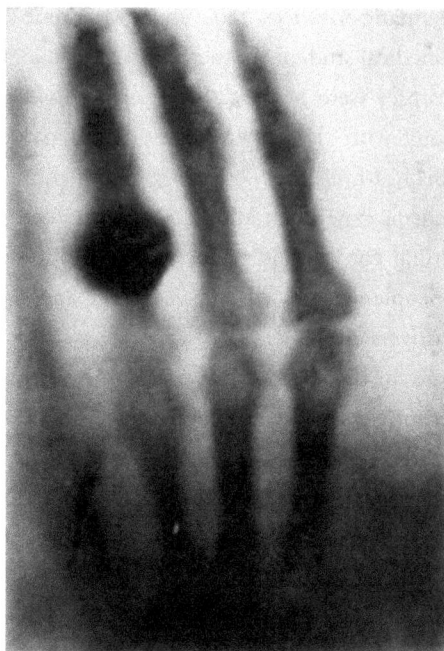

Figure 3.1 The first X-ray, Anna Roentgen's hand showing her wedding ring

Source: Public domain.

of light that could penetrate through solid objects, but their high energy also could destroy chemical bonds in living tissue, altering the structure and functions of cells.

Although poorly understood, radiation now became a new tool with seemingly very promising potential in the medical world's growing arsenal. Radiation was now used, not just for viewing bones and organs beneath the skin (radiology) but also for shrinking and destroying both benign and malignant growths (radiation therapy) such as tumors and cancer cells. In their naiveté and their rush to discover and innovate, the medical profession and the patients they treated didn't realize radiation effects have a slow onset and manifestation of symptoms and these unintended consequences could be severe.

In just a matter of a few years, radiation treatment was seen as a wonder cure as doctors began to use radiation therapy to treat such ailments as acne, ear infections, ringworm, and asthma. With little regulation,

RADIUM
EMANATION WATER
Drives Out Uric Acid

Suffering from too much uric acid and diseases caused by faulty elimination—Rheumatism, Gout, Periodical Headaches, Neuralgia, Constipation, Neurasthenia, Auto-Intoxication and Lack of Bodily Vigor—quickly relieved in a natural way without drugs or chemicals by our new discovery

THE WAY TO MAKE
RADIUM WATER
IN YOUR OWN HOME

with our Rayode. A little device containing Radium enough to supply 2,700 Mache Units of Radio-activity, in two quarts of water every twenty-four hours, for less than 10c a day. The Rayode will last a lifetime.

SEND FOR FREE LITERATURE

Tells how you can buy or rent a Rayode to make Radium Water in your own home, with your own ordinary drinking water. Address:

THE COLORADO RADIUM PRODUCTS COMPANY
635 First National Bank Building   Denver, Colo

Figure 3.2 A typical advertisement of the time marketing the miracle cures of radiation

Source: Public domain.

suddenly, hucksters were exploiting the public's obsession with this new magic potion and began promoting radiation *miracle cures* such as radioactive drinking water, toothpastes, powders, facial creams, and even suppositories.

Affliction: Every Family's Nightmare

For centuries, parents were terrified of what they referred to as *crib death*, which today we call sudden infant death syndrome (SIDS). SIDS occurs without any symptoms or warning signs when a seemingly healthy infant is put down and, for unknown reasons, suddenly dies during their sleep.

In 1889, the Austrian physician, Arnold Paltauf began examining the corpses of SIDS victims and noticed almost all of them appeared to have enlarged thymus glands compared to the cadavers of children he had studied as a medical student and the descriptions detailed in current medical literature. The thymus gland sits behind the breastbone and between the lungs and lies along the trachea, which supplies air to and from the lungs. Relying on the data available to him, Dr. Paltauf concluded that the children he had studied and who died from SIDS had abnormally large thymus glands, and he logically speculated that these enlarged glands were putting pressure on the trachea, causing suffocation as the infants were laid down to sleep. Paltauf named this new ailment *thymicolymphaticus.*

The consensus within the medical community grew as doctors examined infant SIDS victims and observed they appeared to have enlarged thymus glands. Medical specialists began recommending radiation therapy for SIDS in order to reduce the size of the thymus gland. Later, in hopes to preempt thymicolymphaticus from occurring in children, it was recommended by some doctors that all infants should have their thymus gland irradiated to prevent SIDS. It is estimated that thousands of healthy children throughout Europe, Canada, and the United States underwent this procedure.

But the data the researchers were basing such a radical recommendation was not accurate. The SIDS victims that the medical community was currently studying were children of upper- and middle-class families that led relatively comfortable and healthy lifestyles and who could afford medical care. The cadavers of children that they had studied in medical school, their sample population, were all children of the lower class.

What the researchers didn't know, at the time, was that those families living in poor conditions, as the lower class did during the Industrial Revolution, gives rise to a great deal of personal anxiety and this stress—poor diet, squalid conditions, little or no medical care, polluted air, broken families—causes the thymus gland to atrophy and shrink in children.

In effect, they were interpreting their data exactly backward. The upper- and middle-class infants who had larger thymus glands were actually normal and healthy, whereas the sample group they used, the children of the lower-class and poor families, had abnormally small thyroid glands due to their environmental and living conditions. The poor children were anatomically different from the upper- and middle-class children. Thymicolymphaticus never existed. It was a fictitious disease based on a biased sample size.

Conclusion: Paying the Price

By the 1930s, medical researchers slowly began to develop apprehensions about radiating infants for SIDS. As they began to examine more children and young adults of upper- and middle-class families that had died from car accidents, falls, or other accidental deaths other than SIDS, they began to doubt their original observations concerning normal thymus gland size. Also, as medical care began to expand among the poor, researchers were discovering the adverse role stress can play on the human body. In a child, the thymus gland can shrink by one-third after simply a week of enduring stressful conditions.

Despite these new findings, radiation therapy continued in many medical practices until the 1950s when the *father of pediatrics*, Dr. Waldo E. Nelson, published in his classic guide, *Textbook of Pediatrics,* findings showing the thyroid can severely shrink due to environmental stresses and dismissed the idea that it plays any role in SIDS. After decades of irradiating infants, there was no correlation between the size of the thymus gland and sudden infant death syndrome.

The thymus gland is located close to the thyroid, which is particularly sensitive to radiation. Because radiation has a slow onset of symptoms that can take years to manifest, the children treated for SIDS were particularly vulnerable to later contracting thyroid cancer as adults. Female infants were especially endangered due to possibly also contracting breast cancer later in life.

It has been estimated that over 10,000 adults later died from cancer due to the radiation treatment administered to them as infants to prevent SIDS.[1] It has also been assumed that many of the mothers who had held their babies to quiet and calm them during the radiation procedure may have later developed breast cancer.

Closure

In the United States, grave robbing and the resurrectionist trade finally succumbed to public outrage. An early example occurred in 1875 after

---

[1] R.M. Sapolsky. September–October 1991. "Poverty's Remains," *The Sciences.*

former congressman John Scott Harrison passed away in Cincinnati, Ohio. He was the son of American President William Henry Harrison and the father of President Benjamin Harrison. Several days after his burial, his body was quietly deposited in a clandestine drop-off chute in an alley at the Ohio Medical College. Previously, the law looked the other way, realizing it was in the public's best interest to have medical schools learn from stolen cadavers, but seeing such a well-known political figure, from a prominent family, suffering the indignity of grave robbing rather than an unknown pauper caused nationwide public outrage. Soon after, laws were enacted, and states began donating deceased criminals, invalids, and other wards of the state to medical schools. Today, religious and societal outlooks have changed, and medical schools are primarily supplied by private donations. Because of the high price for funeral and burial services, many people donate their bodies, and once examination and study of the cadaver are completed, the schools pay for cremation services and return the remains to the family.

The cause of SIDS is still not fully understood. Current research studies believe there may be a dysfunction within certain infants' brains that controls breathing and arousal from sleep. In the United States, approximately 2,300 babies die of SIDS each year.

Alongside the tragedy of the SIDS cases is the untold number of other children cavalierly treated with radiation therapy for such benign ailments as ringworm, acne, ear infections, asthma, and so on that also paid a very steep price. In the early 1970s, researchers in the United States began to make the connections between childhood radiation and the increase they were seeing in adult cancer patients. Michael Reese Hospital in Chicago was the first to review their records and attempt to locate and notify adults who had been treated as children with radiation therapy. Other hospitals began to follow suit, and in 1977, the National Cancer Institute (NCI) launched a nationwide awareness campaign to encourage anyone who had radiation therapy as a child to get screened for cancer.

Worldwide, it is impossible to determine the number of childhood radiation cases, and there is no valid way to determine how many of these children contracted cancer or died in adulthood due to the radiation administered when they were children. In the United States, alone, an estimated two million children were unnecessarily exposed to radiation for benign conditions.

Chicago Sun-Times film critic Roger Ebert cohosted the popular TV show, *Siskel and Ebert.* His movie reviews were syndicated in over 200 newspapers nationwide, and he was the first movie critic to earn a Pulitzer prize. In 1987, at the age of 45, he was diagnosed and treated for salivary gland cancer. Fifteen years later, he had his thyroid and affected lymph nodes removed. In 2003, the salivary gland cancer returned, and in 2006, cancer had spread to his jaw, which, later, surgeons had to remove. He had a hole inserted in his throat in order to breathe and a tube was placed through his nose to his stomach in order to eat and drink. In 2012, he fell and suffered a broken hip as cancer had spread to his hip bone. Mr. Ebert passed away on April 4, 2013. As a child, he had been treated with high doses of radiation for an ear infection.

Questions to Consider

- Researchers had done their due diligence by comparing the thymus glands of SIDS victims with a control group that was considered to be healthy thymus glands they had studied in medical school journals. They had followed the scientific method and taken reasonable steps to logically reach the conclusion that SIDS victims had abnormally large thymus glands. In reality, are errors like this simply unavoidable?
- At NASA, when one needs to make a critical decision, it is often said, "No data is better than faulty data." The SIDS researchers were using data they trusted to be accurate. It was data published in medical journals and data they had studied in medical school. If this data was faulty, does one have to doubt all data? If so, can one ever confidently make a decision?
- Misinterpreting data or receiving faulty data to make decisions can have long-term effect. For decades after researchers has misdiagnosed the cause of SIDS, infants were still be irradiated for enlarged thymus glands. Can you point out other examples where credible, yet erroneous, decisions

made early on in an engineering design or in a project that had long-term negative effects?

- X-rays and radiation were seen to be life-changing discoveries that had the potential to cure everything from a common cold to cancer. Can researchers and scientists from this era be blamed for not understanding the dangers of radiation before making it widely available to the general public? Is this unusual? Do software producers and car manufacturers release products that are not fully tested and simply use public trials as their test bed?

Case Study: Protecting Allied Planes From Enemy Fire

Abraham Wald was a brilliant Jewish mathematician who immigrated to the United States after the Nazis took over his homeland, Austria, in 1938. When the United States entered World War II, Wald was assigned to the Army's Statistical Research Group (SRG), a classified group of expert mathematicians based out of Columbia University in New York City.

With the Army's Air Corp suffering heavy losses over Europe, the SRG was asked to study aircraft that returned safely from bombing missions over Germany to help determine where extra shielding may be placed to provide better protection against Nazi bullets and flak.

The Army studied the damaged aircraft and, after noticing that most of the holes and damage were located on the lower portion of the fuselage as well as along the wingtips, determined these were the areas that required added reinforcement.

But Wald disagreed. He understood that the conclusions made by the Army officers were the exact opposite of the facts. What they had done was discover the areas of a plane that could take the most hits and still survive. The planes that made it home could withstand damage in the lower fuselage and wingtips—otherwise, they wouldn't have returned. The areas that required extra shielding were the parts of the returned planes that showed little damage, such as the engines, cockpit, and controls.

Wald understood that it was a more complex problem than simply pointing out where the damage was located on the plane. In reality, the planes demonstrated that they could take hits in these areas and survive. One needed to understand that the areas of the plane that showed minor damage were the more fragile parts that needed extra protection from bullets and flak.

In this critical juncture, during the war, Wald's ability to think beyond the obvious evidence saved the lives of countless American airmen. But this isn't an isolated incident, by any means. We tend to dig deep into the data, into the numbers, but sometimes fail to step back and look where the numbers are coming from or how they got there.

Questions for Discussion

- Are there other examples where one needs to look beyond the raw data? For example, I once purchased a new 2.7l Chrysler Sebring, and later discovered it had a serious design flaw. The engine oil passages were drilled too narrow and, after 50,000 to 60,000 miles, these engines tended to develop oil sludge issues that could block these small oil passages, eventually leading to a very expensive repair. After a lot of Internet searches and reading horror stories on Sebring owner's forums, I traded it in. But for many years afterward I continued seeing older, used versions of my Sebring on the roads and highways. I started to believe that all the horror stories I had read on the Internet must have been wrong and, obviously, the 2.7l must have been a dependable engine because here they were 10 to 15 years later still looking quite good.
  What I eventually realized is that the shiny Sebrings I was seeing were cars that owners had invested a lot of money for engine replacements and were now driving them, many years later, to get a return on their repair investment.

- Another simple example of looking beyond the raw data: have you ever walked into a reception area that has a large candy dish and notice the only choices of candy you see are unpopular varieties? Your first thought might be, "Folks in this area sure have a strange fondness for bad candy." In reality, people have already selected the best candy from the dish and left the less popular items for you.

- It is critical to be prepared to look beyond the data, but sometimes, the data is pretty straightforward and says it all. For example, when a football player comes off the field holding his knee, it's very different from Wald inspecting the damaged areas of a bomber. The footballer's knee requires reinforcements not his hip or ankle.

CHAPTER 4

Engineering Ethics and Moral Responsibility

On September 13, 1848, Phineas Gage, a 25-year-old foreman for the Rutland & Burlington Railroad was overseeing a construction crew blasting the granite cliffs along the rolling hills of Cavendish, Vermont. After drilling a hole deep into the rock, a worker would place a dynamite charge into it, add some insulating powder, typically a mixture of sand and clay, and then using a long metal rod, would tamp the charge and powder tight into the hole, as if loading a cannon barrel. At a little past 4 o'clock that afternoon, Phineas Gage found himself standing in the wrong place at the wrong time. Suddenly, the dynamite discharged and the 43-in.-long steel rod weighing over 13 pounds shot out of the blast hole and entered directly under his cheek and exited through the top of his skull. The rod was later found over 90 ft. away.

Incredibly, Phineas not only survived being impaled, but he was still conscious and able to speak. When a doctor arrived, the injured man simply said in his typical self-restrained style, "Doctor, here is business enough for you." Initially, the doctor didn't believe any man could endure such an accident until Phineas started to vomit, and the doctor noticed brain matter oozing from the top of his scalp.

After convalescing for several weeks, Phineas Gage survived with some facial disfigurement and the loss of his left eye. Previously, the young construction foreman was known as outgoing, energetic, well organized, and creative (Gage actually designed the tamping bar that tore through his skull), but now friends, family, and co-workers noticed a starkly different man that was *no longer Gage*. The once even-tempered and unassuming young man was now seen as angry and irascible and described by his attending physician of frequently "indulging at times in the grossest profanity" and possessing "animal passions."

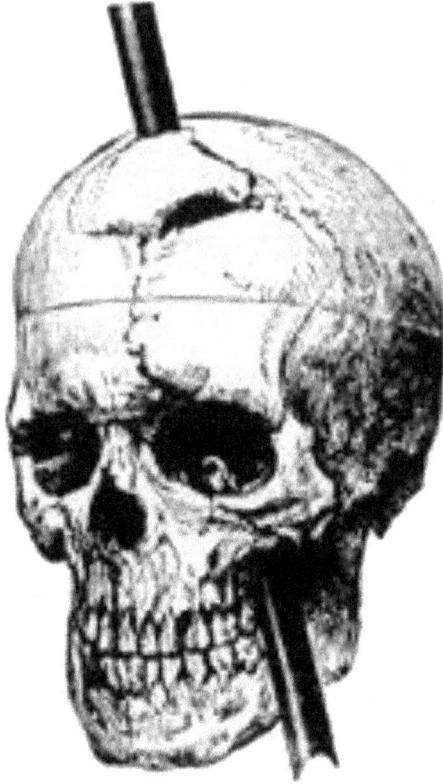

Figure 4.1 19th century depiction of Phineas Gage's injury
Source: Public domain.

What caused such a change in Phineas Gage's personality? The tamping iron that ripped through his skull destroyed his prefrontal cortex. The prefrontal cortex takes up about 10 percent of an adult's brain mass and helps provide the ability to control emotional impulses while also considering the long-term ramifications of one's actions. The prefrontal cortex provides the executive function that is crucial in helping us determine what is right or wrong, good, or bad. Whereas animals are unable to differentiate between right and wrong and ultimately follow the simple path of self-gratification, our prefrontal cortex helps humans ignore impulsive urges and, when necessary, choose the harder, more difficult action because we understand that in the long run, it's the right thing to do.

The prefrontal cortex also provides us with the necessary social skills allowing us to communicate and act in a more acceptable behavior with

Figure 4.2 Phineas Gage posing with the tamping iron that went through his skull

Source: Public domain.

other humans. Many scientists believe the prefrontal cortex evolved in humans to help them work together within a community to survive the ever-present dangers encountered in the ancient natural world.

Primates have a prefrontal cortex, although it is much smaller. In humans, it develops very slowly and isn't fully functional until we reach our mid-20s. In modern, liberal societies, minors are dealt differently under the law because they are too young to fully understand the consequences of their actions. This is an acknowledgment that their prefrontal cortex has not fully matured, and they don't have the same capacity as an adult to recognize right from wrong. Frustrated parents who find themselves constantly correcting their misbehaving children may find some solace knowing that their child's misconduct won't last forever.

Without a prefrontal cortex, Phineas Gage couldn't resume his work at the railroad and, for a short while, traveled New England appearing, with his tamping rod by his side, at events as a human curiosity. For a brief time, he was even on display at the Barnum Museum in New York City. Later, perhaps in a testament to the brain's ability to heal itself, Phineas did find full-time work until, after suffering seizures related to his injury, he finally succumbed at the age of 36 while visiting his mother and sister in San Francisco. Several years later, his body was exhumed, and his skull was removed and shipped back to the physician who had originally cared for him. Today, it, along with the steel rod that passed through it, is on display at the Harvard Medical School's Warren Anatomical Museum in Boston, Massachusetts.

Our Conscience

The horrifying case of Phineas Gage's injury has been used as case study in many neurological and psychological courses and textbooks to describe the function of the prefrontal cortex. This small component differentiates humans from the rest of nature because it provides us with a conscience that allows us to intrinsically know ethical behavior. Your prefrontal cortex is what helps you make the very tough decision to make a substantial personal sacrifice to major in engineering because the future payoff would be worth it. Your prefrontal cortex was also partly responsible for making you feel guilty for copying a friend's homework when you couldn't solve the problem, yourself.

Our brain is an incredibly complex organ, and many regions interact with the prefrontal cortex to help develop what is unique to humankind: a conscience.

Our conscience provides us with some very strong intrinsic moral beliefs. For example, everyone believes that all humans possess individual rights, and they should not be violated. No matter who you are, you are outraged when you hear about a murder or a theft. Even a thief feels he's been wronged when someone steals from him.

But our conscience is not infallible. Sometimes the context—the culture or the era in which a person lives—can affect our moral values. In Mark Twain's classic novel, *The Adventures of Huckleberry Finn*, Huck helps his friend Jim, a fugitive slave, escape on a raft up the Mississippi River. But afterward, Huck is confused, he felt an inner need to help his friend escape but, at the same time, he felt pangs of guilt for enabling another man's property get away, as if he participated in a theft.

Our conscience is also malleable. We can do something we know is wrong but, after continually ignoring our feelings of remorse, our conscience seems to give up and stops bothering us. At NASA, this has sometimes been referred to as, the *normalization of deviance*, a term first coined in Diane Vaughan's classic book, *The Challenger Launch Decision*, in which she describes a series of improper decisions that lead to the catastrophic loss of the shuttle and its seven astronauts. Vaughan details how NASA managers became desensitized after continuing to make dangerous decisions despite knowing the technical risks involved. If it worked before, on a previous flight, despite being a poor design, it should work, again.

In the end, if we ignore our conscience long enough, that uniquely human gift simply stops working, and we relinquish what makes us special and unique.

Morals Versus Ethics

We often use the terms *morality* and *ethics* interchangeably, but there is a difference. Morals are the very strong beliefs by which we try to guide our lives. They feel as if they exist within our very core and are affirmed and strengthened through our family and church. Morals are steadfast, and they seldom change and, if they do, the process is usually very slow, and often very painful.

Whereas as our morals are principles by which we live and we feel are indelible and genuine, ethics are rules imposed by society, or an organization we belong to, that help regulate and administer cooperative behavior among a wide variety of diverse people with diverse beliefs and opinions. Ethics are foundational guidelines that permit orderly interactions among a group of people.

Professional ethics are very clearly defined and are rooted in common sense. For example, the National Society of Professional Engineers (NSPE) puts forth *fundamental canons* by which all professional engineers must adhere to:

1. Hold paramount the safety, health, and welfare of the public
2. Perform services only in areas of their competence

3. Issue public statements only in an objective and truthful manner

4. Act for each employer or client as faithful agents or trustees

5. Avoid deceptive acts

6. Conduct themselves honorably, responsibly, ethically, and lawfully so as to enhance the honor, reputation, and usefulness of the profession[1]

No one is going to argue with these ethical guidelines, and any reasonable person can easily see their validity and practicality.

Although often morals and ethics are complimentary, sometimes they conflict. The classic example of ethics versus morals involves a defense attorney who knows her client is guilty of murder and understands that murder is wrong and immoral but, following the code of legal ethics, attempts to prove her client's innocence before a jury. Another example would be an engineering manager who follows his religious teachings and believes marriage is only allowed between a man and a woman but is assigned an employee who is gay and married. Following his company's code of ethics, the manager must ignore his personal beliefs and treat his gay employee fairly and without prejudice. In essence, your company is paying you to provide a pluralistic and fair workplace by keeping your personal and religious beliefs separate from the organization's ethics.

We may follow the ethical guidelines stated by the NSPE, or other professional organizations, but still find ourselves facing a moral dilemma. For a technical person, ethics and morality may be described as the difference between *complicated* and *complex*. Designing a rocket, building a nuclear reactor, or constructing a skyscraper are *complicated* endeavors but we have rules and equations for developing these complicated projects and, if we follow them, we will have success. We are trained to solve complicated problems. But sometimes we are faced with a *complex* problem that doesn't come with an instruction manual, assembly diagram, or handy equations. Raising a baby is complex. We don't know what the rules are and it's complex on both ends![2] Using our analytical skills, we are very good at solving

---

[1] www.nspe.org/resources/ethics/code-ethics.

[2] I owe this complex/complicated analogy to Rev. Michael Cavanagh, a colleague who attended our Fifth Year Forum.

complicated problems but, unfortunately, moral choices don't always follow such a simple, or clear logical approach. They are complex.

An example of moral complexity can be found in Victor Hugo's timeless masterpiece, *Les Miserables*, when Jean Valjean, a man who finds himself trapped in a society being torn apart by rebellion and cholera epidemic. He tries but cannot find work and, in desperation, has to steal a loaf of bread in order to feed his starving family. Valjean has committed a crime, he has done an immoral and unethical act by stealing property that does not belong to him. For this crime, Valjean spends most of his life hiding as he is ruthlessly and ceaselessly hunted down by the Paris policeman, Javert.

Was Jean Valjean wrong for stealing bread for his family? Was the policeman, Javert, wrong for doing the job he was paid to do? A complex situation, indeed.

Data and Values

Most technical people are more comfortable dealing with objective facts that are not debatable. So, when dealing with morality and values, which are personal beliefs and cannot be analytically proven valid or nonvalid, it can become somewhat more difficult for an engineer to make a complex judgment.

We love data, but there's more to life than simply determining facts. The Danish philosopher, Kierkegaard, told a story of a person who escaped from a lunatic asylum. In order not to appear suspicious and get caught, the man decided to change his behavior, and if approached, he would only speak facts rather than rambling on incoherently as he'd previously done. Inevitably, he encounters several people as he walks throughout the town and, hoping to seem normal and inconspicuous, simply states objective facts as, "The sun is out." "The world is round." "The sky is blue." By simply speaking only facts, the man proves he is insane, and the townsfolks call a police officer who escorts him back to the asylum.

Data and facts are everywhere, we are inundated, but in order for *facts* to be useful, they must contain something we *value*.

For example, NASA has spent over two decades and over 10 billion dollars developing the James Webb Space Telescope (JWST) that, once launched and positioned over a million miles from earth, will be able to see the universe almost back to the Big Bang. Obviously, we have the skill and the expertise to build, launch, and deploy such incredibly *complicated* machines, but why do we do it? Why do we exert such an enormous effort and spend huge amounts of money on a technical device that will describe the universe? JWST is not going to make life easier for anyone on earth, it's not going to make anyone a profit, it's not going to cure poverty, or end global warming, or end war, but it will give us more knowledge of our universe. Of course, we want to end poverty and so on, but we also *value* knowledge. We are willing to work for decades and spend billions of dollars because we have a fundamental human desire, a passion to understand how the universe works and how we got here, because we *value* this knowledge.

You cannot make a decision on facts alone, you must include value, and placing a value means you must be willing to make a *judgment*. For an engineer or any technical person, this now becomes *complex*.

Almost everything an engineer designs involves a judgment and includes values because it involves the health and safety of those customers who will use it. In every design, an engineer is faced with making a decision that involves a compromise, and a risk, and thus becomes a question of value.

When we build a car, there are severe engineering restraints that involve questions of safety. An automobile could be designed to permit its occupants to withstand a head-on collision at 50 miles per hour, but such a car would weigh so much it would get terrible gas mileage and be so unsightly that it would be impossible to market. When an automotive engineer designs a car, he/she places a value on human life. The customer demands good fuel economy, sporty looks, so the engineer has to reduce weight and, thus, reduce the safety of the vehicle, which increases the risk of injury or even death to the consumer. The design engineer has made complex moral judgments based on values.

Moral decision making is as integral to engineering as calculus because each engineering decision involves just as much math as it does risk. Recall the anonymous quote often cited by civil engineers: "Any idiot can build a bridge that stands but it takes an engineer to build a bridge that barely stands."

Why Ethics Are Important for STEM

Engineering and technology occupy a unique place in modern society. Engineers, technicians, and architects possess the skills most others lack—they know how to transform dreams into reality. Engineers can convert a dry, infertile valley into farmland by constructing a dam to provide irrigation; engineers have made the dream of flight a reality; architects have constructed buildings that can reach thousands of feet into the sky. But these same technical gifts can also turn dreams into nightmares when judgments are made and values are ignored.

Ferdinand Porsche, the engineer who designed the Volkswagen (VW)—an automobile that revolutionized personal travel for the common man—also designed one of the most terrifying battle tanks that helped kill over 20 million Russians on the Eastern Front. Werner Von Braun, who designed, built, and launched the V-2 rockets that terrorized London in the waning months of the Second World War was the same engineer who designed, built, and launched the Saturn V rocket that enabled the United States to land a man on the Moon. Both Porsche and Von Braun were following the ethical codes of the professional engineer when they were designing tanks and missiles but ignored the *complex* moral values of their age.

Technical people, such as architects and engineers, have a unique power within society by turning a concept or an idea into reality. We all too often take these abilities for granted and seldom realize that, for the nontechnical, this skill appears to be almost miraculous. The British novelist, Arthur C. Clarke, once said that, "Any sufficiently advanced technology is indistinguishable from magic."[3] The skills to build a skyscraper, a computer, or place a man on the moon certainly appear to be magic to the layperson. Technical people, alone, possess this power of modern-day magic and must safeguard that inner voice—their conscience—that originates from the prefrontal cortex to guide them in making proper judgments based on foundational human values.

---

[3] A.C. Clarke. 1961. *Profiles of The Future* (Known as Clarke's third law).

Recognizing a Moral Situation

How to know if you're faced with a moral situation or question? Here are some questions to ask yourself:

- Who is going to benefit? If it's just you, that's a big warning.
- Who will be hurt, suffer from your decision? A co-worker for daring to question you? A rival for a promotion?
- Would you make the same decision if you were in the other person's shoes?
- How would you advise a loved one that found themselves in a similar situation?
- Is this a struggle between what is right or what is expedient?
- Are you being transparent or hiding your thoughts and decisions?

When making an ethical decision, consider:

- Is this the kind of world you want to live in?
- Would you give your children the same advice?
- Is this how you want to be remembered?
- Look at the people you hold in esteem. What would they do?
- Will it be worth the price you're going to pay? Remember, nothing in life is free, even the decisions we make.
- Once you make your decision, in your heart you will always know if you acted in a noble way. Can you live with the decision you made?

As an engineering manager and leader:

- Your character is the single most important asset you have in the business world. Is this decision going to jeopardize your reputation?
- Trust has to be earned; once it is lost, you may never get it back. Will you lose the hard-earned trust of your co-workers and colleagues?

- Ethical decisions in the workplace are critical, and you may face legal action if you haven't done your due diligence.
- As a leader, you represent your company. If your team believes their organization is ethical, they are much more likely to also act and behave in an ethical manner.
- And also, if your team believes their organization is unethical, they are much more likely to act in an unethical manner.
- And, if your team doesn't know what their organization stands for, it can create confusion and/or paralysis.

I once participated in a brainstorming session with a group of engineers who were discussing the incredibly complicated mission to land astronauts on Mars. As with all things that fly or move, weight considerations must be taken into place. There are rockets big enough to carry astronauts and all the necessary supplies on a three-month journey to Mars—it's returning the humans from Mars back to Earth that is the difficult engineering task. There is no fuel on Mars, so in order to return the astronauts, they would have to carry huge amounts of fuel from Earth all the way to Mars for the return trip. With this additional weight, it would be impossible for current rockets to launch from Earth on a trip to Mars, and to design and build a new rocket capable of such a heavy payload would require a gargantuan rocket with an equally gargantuan cost. After countless hours of discussions and feasibility conversations, one very brilliant engineer stated, what many were already thinking, "Why don't we ask for volunteers who would be willing to be launched to Mars to conduct a variety of experiments and scientific explorations on the surface with the understanding that they eventually will run out of food and supplies and be left to die on the Martian surface? They would be viewed as a paragon for future explorers because of their willingness to sacrifice their lives for the advancement of science." A complicated engineering task suddenly got very complex.

Consider all this; and then turn to this green, gentle, and most docile earth. Consider them both, the sea and the land; and do you not find a strange analogy to something in yourself? For as this appalling ocean surrounds the verdant land, so in the soul of man there lies an insular

Tahiti, full of peace and joy, but encompassed by all the horrors of the half known life. God keep thee! Push not off from that isle, thou canst never return!

—Herman Melville *Moby Dick*

Suggested Resources

Brown, B.J. n.d. "The Building of a Virtuous Transformational Leader." www .regent.edu/acad/global/publications/jvl/vol2_iss1/Brown_JVLV2I1_p6-14. pdf.

Grim, P. 2005. "Questions of Value." The Teaching Company.

Kidder, R. 2009. "How Good People Make Tough Choices: Resolving the Dilemmas of Ethical Living." Harper Perennial.

Kreeft, P. 2008. "Ethics: A History of Moral Thought." Modern Scholar.

Markos, L. 2000. "The Life and Writings of C. S. Lewis." The Teaching Company.

Mazzeo, G. 2019. "Sleeping Dogs: Ethics in the Workplace." Independently Published.

Nelson, K.A. and L.K. Trevino. 2010. "Managing Business Ethics: Straight Talk About How to Do it Right." Wiley.

Sereny, G. 1996. "Albert Speer: His Battle With Truth." Vintage.

Speer, A. 1995. "Inside the Third Reich." Bbs Pub Corp.

Case Study: Dieselgate

Volkswagen AG, headquartered in Wolfsburg, Germany, makes several different brands of autos, but the most well-known are the VW, Audi, and Porsche nameplates. In 2008, VW was the largest automobile manufacturer in Europe and the third biggest in the world behind only Toyota and General Motors. That same year, VW introduced *Strategy 2018*, setting an ambitious goal utilizing their diesel expertise to become the world's largest automobile company within a decade.

With a particular focus on Toyota and its fuel-efficient line of hybrid vehicles that were becoming increasingly popular in the lucrative U.S. market, company executives were determined to develop an all-new diesel engine that could not only compete with such Toyota offerings as the Prius on fuel efficiency and environmental cleanliness but would surpass hybrids, well known for their poor performance, on power and acceleration.

But in 2015, the company's plan for domination of the automobile market became derailed when three mechanical engineering graduate students at West Virginia University (WVU) noticed an anomaly between the emissions measurements of several VW models during real-world driving conditions compared to lab results. Before long, these significantly differing readings were traced to a covert code lurking in the VW emissions control computer. Suddenly, just as VW was hoping to cross the Strategy 2018 finish line, the company became embroiled in the largest corporate fraud in history.

The Turbocharged Direct Injection (TDI) Engine

Diesel engines have a long history in the European market. Because of their exceptional fuel economy, a diesel engine emits less carbon dioxide (CO_2) per mile than a gasoline internal combustion engine. European politicians saw this as an answer to concerns over climate change and greenhouse gasses, which have been directly related to CO_2 emissions. The European Union has further supported diesel cars by taxing gasoline at a higher rate than diesel fuel and as well as discounting diesel car registrations. The European auto manufacturers supported these policies knowing they already had in place a substantial manufacturing infrastructure to develop diesel cars.

Diesels are more fuel efficient and do have a smaller carbon footprint compared to internal combustion engines, but they do pollute significant amounts more of nitrogen oxide (NOx) and particulate matter. NOx has been shown to be one of the primary causes for smog that plagues cities and also can cause severe respiratory ailments in humans.

In the United States, the Environmental Protective Agency (EPA) and the California Air Resource Board (CARB) have a different focus toward auto emissions than their European counterparts. Whereas European politicians seek to stem the effects of global warming, American regulators focus on clean air standards, particularly smog, which is caused primarily by NOx emissions from automobiles and is a continual hazard for large congested cities, particularly in California where the mountains can act as a barrier trapping smog to the point where it obstructs visibility.

The engineers at VW were given a daunting task of designing a four-cylinder diesel that could meet American emission standards. If they could do it, VW could challenge hybrids by having a small carbon footprint with exceptional fuel mileage while beating it with more power and acceleration. If successful, the VW engineering team had the opportunity to see their company ascend to the biggest car maker in the world.

VW designers developed the all new TDI, a turbocharged, direct fuel injection four cylinder that was installed in numerous VW models such as the popular Beetle, Jetta, and Golf. As U.S. and Japanese manufacturers began banking on hybrids to gain market share, VW bet on the diesel. VW proudly touted their new offering with an expansive marketing campaign, including reaching out to huge audiences during the Super Bowl.

WVU Mountaineers Hit the Road

In California, where emissions restrictions are even tighter than the EPA's, CARB was puzzled that environmental testing of VW products was showing significant anomalies. They reached out to a group of researchers at WVU to help solve the mystery. Three grad students, Arvind Thiruvengadam, Hemanth Kappanna, and Marc Besch, borrowed several VW cars, equipped them with emissions monitoring equipment, and set off

This ain't your daddy's diesel.

Stinky, smoky, and sluggish. Those old diesel realities no longer apply. Enter TDI Clean Diesel. Ultra-low-sulfur fuel, direct injection technology, and extreme efficiency.   We've ushered in a new era of diesel.

• Engineered to burn low-sulfur diesel fuel
• "Common Rail" direct injection system

View key fuel efficiency info ?

Figure 4.3 Volkswagen's marketing campaign for the TDI engine
Source: VW advertisement.

along the California highways. What they discovered was that the TDI equipped cars were releasing up to 40 times the permitted amount of NOx gasses. The readings were so far off the trio of young engineers thought their equipment faulty. Pulled off the side of the California highways to clean and recalibrate, they had to explain themselves to curious highway patrolmen. But again, the readings were showing NOx emissions well above those permitted by the state of California and the EPA.

German Engineering: The Defeat Device

VW engineers couldn't meet U.S. pollution guidelines and still provide good gas mileage and acceleration. The compromise they faced involved the NOx trap on the TDI. In order for the trap to work effectively, that is, pass U.S. pollution regulations, it required the engine to burn more fuel, thus decreasing fuel mileage as well as acceleration, thereby canceling the very advantage VW was hoping for in a diesel. As one VW manager said, "The CARB is not realistic. We can do quite a bit… But (the) impossible, we cannot do."

The sophisticated software algorithm was designed to recognize when the car was being placed on an emissions control dynamometer. That is, the car's sensors could detect when the drive wheels were rotating while the other wheels were stationary and the steering wheel was held constant in a straight position. When the computer detected these inputs, it would send commands to the NOx trap, increasing its effectiveness but also causing more fuel to be burned, thus allowing the TDI to pass the test. Once the computer recognized that the automobile was removed from the dynamometer, it returned the engine to the default settings, burning less fuel, lowering the NOx trap's effectiveness, and increasing allowable NOx emission well above the regulated limits.

The engineers at VW found themselves in an all too familiar spot, they were expected to deliver on unrealistic, and in this case, impossible, promises made by marketing and supported by upper management.

German Engineer: Oliver Schmidt

Oliver Schmidt was born in Lower Saxony where VW was headquartered and where it employed more than 100,000 people. VW is to Lower Saxony as GM is to Detroit, but on steroids. After graduating as a mechanical engineer and performing his military service, Oliver got his dream job and joined VW in 1997. He was a committed and loyal employee to the company, and in his spare time, he would rebuild old VW Beetles in his garage. When he married his wife, another VW engineer, they hosted the ceremony in a friend's VW dealership.

In 2005, Schmidt was recognized as a brilliant engineer with a solid future and was selected with several other gifted employees to join team *Moonraker*. They were sent to the United States to integrate themselves within society to see what Americans like, to understand their culture and needs, and to bring this knowledge back to Wolfsburg where it could be used to better market VW cars in the United States. As he traveled across America, Schmidt later wrote, "Over the eighteen months I spent there, I learned a lot... I also fell more in love with America." Schmidt was moving up the corporate ladder.

In 2012, Oliver Schmidt was promoted to General Manager in charge of the Environmental and Engineering Office stationed outside Detroit in Auburn Hills, Michigan. In this role, with a salary of $170,000, he was responsible for communicating and coordinating with regulatory agencies such as the EPA and CARB. Schmidt and his wife purchased property in Florida with the dream of someday retiring in the United States.

Events Move Slowly, Then Very Quickly

In May of 2014, the EPA started pressing VW for answers concerning the discrepancies discovered by the WVU team. VW's response, led by Schmidt, was an attempt to stonewall the agencies with promises of recalls and simple software fixes. For more than a year, VW's strategy worked.

Schmidt was well aware of the defeat device. When he was originally informed that the U.S. regulators had discovered anomalies and were raising questions, he e-mailed a colleague in Germany, "It should first be decided whether we are (to be) honest. If we are not (going to be) honest, everything stays as it is…"

In May 2015, Oliver Schmidt was promoted again and returned to Wolfsburg to become Principal Deputy to the Head of Engine Development. On several occasions, Schmidt briefed management on the gathering storm back in the United States. In corporate boardrooms, Schmidt described the potential for enormous costs involved in actually fixing the TDI equipped cars as well as the possibility of the U.S. government issuing criminal indictments. Company officials tasked the loyal and dutiful Schmidt with returning to the United States to use whatever personal influence he may have to minimize the scandal and to continue to mislead the regulators but without revealing the existence of the defeat device. While Schmidt honed his strategy, he had doubts about one of his team members when another VW manager warned him that an engineer (unnamed and known only as *Cooperating Witness 1* in the Criminal Complaint filed in the U.S. District Court) "… should not come along [to the CARB meeting] so he would not have to consciously lie."

But upon arrival at the CARB offices in California in August 2015, the VW engineer, (*Cooperating Witness 1*), who was feeling remorse for his role in the deception and didn't feel comfortable lying to government officials, described the TDI's defeat device to stunned U.S. regulators.

On September 3, 2015, realizing they had no other choice available, VW management admitted that the defeat devices existed and had been installed on almost 600,000 diesel cars sold in the United States as well as 11 million more sold worldwide.

On September 18, the EPA issued a Notice of Violation to VW for failure to comply with the U.S. Clean Air Act, effectively stopping all sales of VW diesels in the United States.

Five days later, the CEO of VW, Martin Winterkorn, who was the highest paid CEO in Germany with a salary of 18.6 million dollars, and a notorious micromanager who carried a pair of micrometers with him when visiting assembly plants to personally verify part tolerances, resigned stating, "I am doing this in the interests of the company even though I am not aware of any wrongdoing on my part." Within days, VW stock dropped 30 percent.

In October 2015, VW's American CEO, Michael Horn, was summoned before a congressional house oversight committee. He claimed that a group of *rogue software engineers* were responsible for the defeat device, and that VW management was unaware of its existence until a month ago. Rep. Jan Schakowsky (D-Ill.) said, "The company's word isn't worth a dime."

In October of 2016, VW agreed to a 14.7 billion dollars settlement to compensate car owners and as punishment for environmental damage. By 2018, the cumulative cost to VW, including fines, lawsuits, fixes, and car buy-back programs, had reached a staggering 30 billion dollars. To put this in perspective, you could have built 25 of Dallas' enormous, new AT&T stadium with the cost of Dieselgate. NASA's 2018 budget was 19.1 billion dollars.

Across the United States lie 37 VW *graveyards* where thousands of diesel-powered autos bought back from angry customers can still be seen in such areas as the Pontiac Silverdome and the Port of Baltimore.

Who Paid a Price … and Who Didn't?

In January 2016, Schmidt and his wife vacationed at their Florida condo. When their Christmas holiday ended, they prepared to return to Germany. At the Miami airport, Schmidt was followed by eight federal agents as he entered the men's room, and when he came out, he was wearing handcuffs and his wife was left sobbing at the airport gate.

After Schmidt saw the evidence against him, he pled guilty, telling Judge Sean F. Cox in a letter, "I've learned that my superiors that claimed to me to have not been involved earlier than me at VW knew about this for many, many years. I must say that I feel misused by my own company."

Judge Cox had previously sentenced another VW executive embroiled in Dieselgate and expressed the gravity he saw in the scandal stating, "This is a very serious and troubling crime against our economic system. Without that trust in corporate America, the economy can't function."

Despite an enormous outpouring of personal references from friends and colleagues that impressed Judge Cox, he remained firm and sentenced Schmidt to seven years imprisonment. He reminded Schmidt that as a judge, he has a solemn duty to uphold justice even when he's confronted with "good people just making very, very bad decisions."

The judge told Schmidt he had committed his crime "to impress senior management…" Adding, "You saw this as an opportunity to shine … and climb the corporate ladder." Judge Cox intended the stiff sentence to be seen as a deterrent to others who may become tempted to place their loyalty to a company above the law.

Figure 4.4 Oliver Schmidt mugshot after his arrest
Source: Broward County Sherriff Office.

Standing before the judge after sentencing, with tears in his eyes and choking on his words, Schmidt read a statement:

> For the disruption to my own life, I only have to blame myself. The hardest part is knowing the pain I have caused to those who love me most, most especially my wife Kerstin, who dropped everything to move from Germany to the U.S. to be closer to me, so we can continue to support one another as we have done for the past 20 years.
>
> I accept responsibility for the wrongs I committed. ...I made bad decisions and for that I am sorry. For a time, I was in denial that I personally did something wrong. I justified my bad decisions by telling myself that I was obligated to stick to my superiors' instructions.
>
> Sitting here today it is of course easy to say what I could have or should have done differently. ...I wish I did do things differently, but none of that is of any use. I am deeply sorry for the wrongs I committed, and I am as ready as I will ever be to accept the punishment you believe is just and fair.

For Oliver Schmidt, VW had been his passion, his life, his religion. Now he was alone. The archetype loyal employee, the brilliant engineer who had devoted everything to VW and always did his duty now felt betrayed as a scapegoat and fall guy for many others higher than him on the corporate ladder. To accentuate his nightmare, he felt humiliated to see his mugshot as the emblem of the scandal.

Preamble to the National Society of Professional Engineers Code of Ethics

...engineers are expected to exhibit the highest standards of honesty and integrity. Engineering has a direct and vital impact on the quality of life for all people. Accordingly, the services provided by engineers require honesty, impartiality, fairness, and equity, and must be dedicated to the protection of the public health, safety, and welfare. Engineers must perform under a standard of professional behavior that requires adherence to the highest principles of ethical conduct.

Das Ende

After the scandal, VW desperately wanted a new image. The company dumped their familiar marketing slogan *Das Auto* now synonymous with Dieselgate and looked for a more *humble* marketing theme. For their shareholders, they introduced *Strategy 2025* a new effort to invest billions of euros to become the leading manufacturer of electric vehicles worldwide. The company's stock has mostly recovered, and VW is now the second leading carmaker in the world behind, of course, Toyota. In Europe, VW has never paid out a euro for the 8.5 million TDIs sold, claiming that even with the cheat device their cars still met European Union (EU) standards; therefore, they never broke any laws. Diesel sales in Europe have plummeted as politicians reconsider their existing pollution standards, and potential buyers shun them over fears of lower resale values. VW no longer sells diesels in the United States.

On October 13, 2017, the three West Virginia University grad students, Arvind Thiruvengadam, Hemanth Kappanna, and Marc Besch, who unwittingly uncovered the greatest fraud in corporate history, were honored by roaring crowds as grand marshals during homecoming weekend when their alma mater played Texas Tech. WVU won, 46-35.

On May 3, 2018, Martin Winderkorn, VW's former CEO, was formally charged in a U.S. court for fraud and conspiracy. U.S. prosecutors allege he was briefed during the meeting with Oliver Schmidt in Wolfsburg in 2015 about the defeat device and approved continuing to conceal it from U.S. regulators. It's doubtful, Winderkorn, or any other VW employees, will ever be prosecuted because Germany seldom extradites accused citizens outside of the EU. American prosecutors feel he, and others involved in the scandal, are being protected by the influence of a company that represents German pride as well as a company that is 20 percent owned by the state of Lower Saxony.

Oliver Schmidt was fired from VW and is currently serving his sentence in the Federal Corrections Institute in Milan, Michigan. When released in 2023, he will be immediately deported to Germany and required to pay 400,000 dollars in restitution to the U.S. government. Oliver Schmidt will not be retiring to Florida.

Questions to Consider

- By all accounts, Oliver Schmidt, was considered a good man—he served his country, was a good husband, and was a smart and hardworking employee. What caused Schmidt to become embroiled in this scandal? Money? Career growth? Company loyalty?
- From the section above, *Recognizing a Moral Situation*, which questions might have made Schmidt reconsider his involvement in the scandal?
- As Arthur C. Clarke said, "Any sufficiently advanced technology is undistinguishable from magic." Is this a case where VW thought they could outsmart the regulators and the public? In retrospect, did they ever have a chance?
- How could individual managers from an internationally respected corporation like VW convince themselves what they were attempting was not wrong?

Case Study: SCE to AUX. Is It Ever Permissible to Lie?

Is it ever permissible to tell a lie? Philosophers have been debating this for centuries. Here's some opinions:

- Plato: Yes, in *The Republic*, Plato's utopia is administered by an elite cabal of *philosopher-kings* who can tell a *noble lie* to the less enlightened citizens in order to maintain order and control. On a more personal level, we may tell an ill family member that everything is going to be all right, even though we know their illness is terminal.

- Immanuel Kant: Under no circumstances, is it ever permissible to tell a lie. For Kant, a moral absolutist, humans are uniquely special because they possess reason. Our reason can only work accurately if it has the correct information. If someone tells you a falsehood, it prevents you from knowing the real truth and therefore clouds your ability to make a proper, well-informed decision.

- John Stuart Mill: Mill followed a philosophy known as *Utilitarianism*. If something beneficial occurs from lying, then it is acceptable lie. An example would be telling a friend to come over for dinner when, in reality, you have invited him over to conduct a drug or alcohol intervention session.

- Machiavelli: Yes, it is permissible to lie, when convenient. Machiavelli believed one's ethics were dependent upon the situation. Lying is acceptable if it's the most practical way to achieve one's goals. Practicality is the Machiavellian foundation. The world of politics is strewn with Machiavellian examples.

On November 14, 1969, at 11:23 a.m., the crew of Apollo 12, Pete Conrad, Dick Gordon, and Allan Bean, lifted off the pad at the Kennedy Space Center on its way to America's second moon landing. That Friday morning had seen significant cloud cover as well as recurrent rain showers but was still within the launch commit criteria. Just 36 seconds after launch, commander Pete Conrad exclaimed, "What the hell was that?" and saw a streak of light outside the command module's window. As the massive Saturn V was lumbering its way through the clouds, it was struck by a bolt of lightning. The strike caused warning lights and buzzers to light up the control panel within their command module as all three fuel cells powering the capsule went offline. Conrad told Mission Control, "Okay, we just lost the platform, gang, we had everything in the world drop out."

In Houston, flight controllers were desperately trying to ascertain the condition of the spacecraft and determine how to get it back online. Fortunately, Saturn V's guidance control computer was not damaged, and the huge rocket remained fully powered and on the correct trajectory. As flight director Gerry Griffin was contemplating aborting the mission, a 26-year-old flight controller, John Aaron, in charge of electrical, environmental and consumables, came forward and suggested the astronauts try *SCE to AUX*, a hitherto unknown command that no one in mission control recognized. When it was relayed to Conrad, he was puzzled, having never heard of it. Fortunately, astronaut Al Bean knew where the obscure *SCE to AUX* switch was located, flipped it, and suddenly the command module came back to life and astronaut Gordon shouted, "God darn Almighty, wasn't that something!"

But back at mission control, some engineers were concerned there may still be some aftereffects from the lightning strike, particularly on the pyrotechnic bolts located above the command module that, upon

Figure 4.5 Lightning storm that hit Apollo 12 also struck the launch tower immediately after lift-off

Source: NASA.

re-entry in the earth's atmosphere, fire and release the parachutes to slow the capsule before landing in the ocean. Some engineers feared the strike may have prematurely fired the bolts, which would be catastrophic for the crew upon splashdown.

It was decided at mission control not to tell the astronauts of their concerns. There was no way to verify the integrity of the pyrotechnic bolts, and if they had fired, there was simply nothing anyone could do to fix them. There's little reason to abort the mission, now, and de-orbit if they were unsure of the bolts so might as well continue with the mission objectives. Telling the astronauts might cause such anxiety that they may make fatal mistakes as the mission included a technically difficult lunar landing. With the astronauts safely in earth orbit and all the systems checked out nominal, mission control gave them permission for the trans-lunar injection burn (TLI), and they were on their way to the moon.

Later analysis discovered that the huge exhaust plume generated by the Saturn V had ionized and, in effect, transformed the rocket into a conducting rod as it passed through the electrically charged clouds to the earth.

Apollo 12 did successfully land on the moon, and the engineers' fears about the bolts proved unwarranted as the capsule successfully landed on November 24, splashing down in the Pacific Ocean.

Something similar, although much more catastrophic happened to the Space Shuttle, Columbia, when NASA managers discovered tiles may have hit and damaged the shuttle on launch. Managers decided not to tell the crew of the possible dangers, again because they felt there was nothing that could be done, and it would most likely affect the attitude and behavior of the astronauts on their mission. But others have come back and said, it also prevented an *Apollo 13 moment* when a team of brilliant engineers at Mission Control successfully accomplished the impossible and saved the crew after a helium tank exploded. Morton Thiokol's Allan J. McDonald, who years earlier tried to convince NASA not to launch the doomed Challenger said this about the Columbia disaster, "It was the first time in NASA's 50-year history that I saw they went from a 'can do' attitude to a 'can't do' and that was the most serious mistake, most unethical mistake made in their entire history."[4]

---

[4] www.youtube.com/watch?v=QbtY_Wl-hYI.

Questions to Consider

- Was mission control right to keep their concerns about the pyrotechnic fasteners from the crew?
- If you had been on Apollo 12, would you have wanted to know about the engineers' concerns over the bolts? If you were told, would it have impacted your work on the flight?
- If you were an astronaut sitting in mission control witnessing flight controllers purposely keeping these safety concerns from the crew, would it effect your trust in them when you flew?
- For an engineering manager to abort any mission such as an Apollo moon landing or Space Shuttle flight involves measuring the risk to the astronauts with the enormous program costs in funding and manpower, the organization's reputation, along with the real probability existing in the technical failure encountered. Is this simply an engineering cost/benefit ratio discussion or is it a judgment of value?

Case Study: Albert Speer and the Danger of the Technocrat

More certain, too, that the barbarians are not only at the door, that they are inside us. And that a sense of measure, of compassion, of fundamental decency is the product of careful nurture which can be erased by a private megalomania, fusing with public megalomania, releasing when it does, all that is bloody-minded in the human race.

—Helen Wolff [5]

Historian Theodore Roszak has famously stated that scientists and technologists view the world *through the eyes of a dead man.*[6] Roszak refers to the disturbing quality that afflicts many technical people—an overriding focus on pragmatism and efficiency at the expense of more humane values. It is the inherent nature of the technical disciplines that forces its practitioners to view the world with a practical eye and possess a preoccupation with efficiency and order.

But the latent danger for any engineer is to become so absorbed in this engineering mindset as to lose touch with nonanalytical and the non-computational side of life. Although the technical mindset encourages practicality and efficiency above all, such an unrestricted viewpoint may unintentionally transform the talented and unemotional engineer into a human being with a restricted, and potentially dangerous, *Weltanschauung.*[7] In his book, *The Civilized Engineer*, Samual Florman describes the typical characteristics of an engineer: cautious, hard-working, dependable, orderly, pragmatic, and overly serious.[8] Such personal qualities may be necessary to be a successful engineer, but left unchecked and unbalanced by other, more *humane* attributes, they also pose a dangerous risk when they further transform the technical person into one who views the world with *the eyes of a dead man.*

[5] W. Kempowski. 1975. *Did You Ever See Hitler?* (Avon Books), Preface.

[6] T. Roszak. 1987. *Where the Wasteland Ends* (Celestial Arts), p. 328.

[7] From the New Oxford American Dictionary: *Weltanschauung*—a particular philosophy or view of life; the worldview of an individual or group.

[8] S.C. Florman. 1987. *The Civilized Engineer* (St. Martin's Griffin), Ch. 5.

Perhaps no man better exemplifies this danger than Albert Speer—Hitler's architect and Minister of Armaments. Speer possessed the analytical skills and personal characteristics of Florman's typical engineer and combined them with an outlook toward life that is beyond simply amoral—something even more sinister and potentially dangerous. Speer's elusive persona was probably best described by the author, Gitta Sereny, who got to know Speer better than any other person in his life, yet she never really felt she *knew* him: "...I felt neither the Nuremberg trial nor [Speer's] book told us...how a man of such quality could become not immoral not amoral but, somehow infinitely worse, morally extinguished."[9]

Speer personified the extreme case of what can happen when a brilliant technical mind is coupled with a disinterest in ethics and morality. Engineers, architects, and technicians provide a benefit to society by designing and constructing countless systems, services, and products but unless they also possess a firm grounding in ethics, morality, and the lessons of history their brilliant technical minds can easily be manipulated by the evil forces both from outside them and from within them.

Someone designed the furnaces of the Nazi death camps. Someone measured the size and weight of a human corpse to determine how many could be stacked and efficiently incinerated within a crematorium. Someone, very well educated, sketched out on a drafting table the simulated hot water spigots within the huge de-contamination showers that were treacherously used at Auschwitz to entice innocent victims to their deaths. Someone designed the rooftop openings and considered their optimum placement for the Zyklon B pellets to be dropped among the naked, helpless men, women, and children below.[10]

---

[9] G. Sereny. 1995. *Albert Speer, His Battle With Truth* (Random House), p. 10.

[10] The caption for the architectural drawing in Figure 4.6 reads: "Plate 18: Final design for crematorium IV, by Walther Dejaco, January 1943. Original blueprint, Auschwitz-Birkenau State Museum, box BW (B) 30b; redrawn for publication by Mikolaj Kadlubowski. The center of the incineration room is occupied by a double-four-muffle furnace connected to two chimneys. The section through the lower part of the building shows one of the two gas chambers, the chimney of the stove of the other gas chamber, and the corridor. The section through the higher part of the building shows the furnace room." (*Dwork & Van Pelt, between 320-21*)

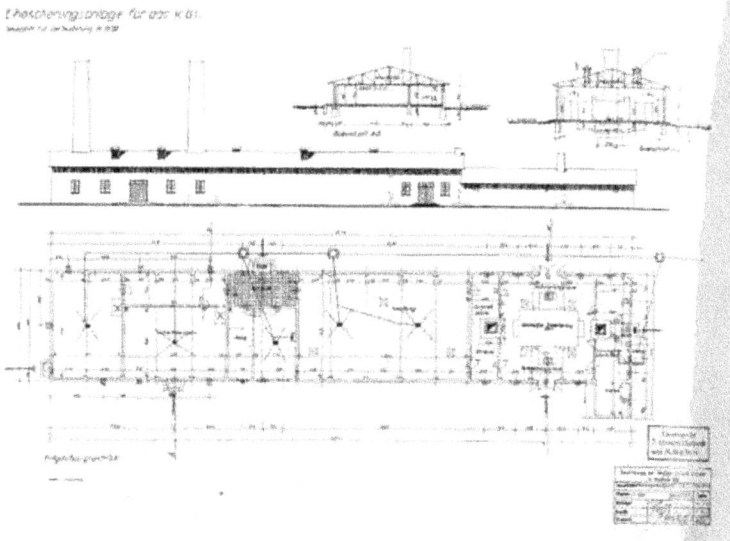

Figure 4.6 Architectural drawing of the crematorium at Auschwitz
Source: www.jewishvirtuallibrary.org.

This person was an engineer, an architect, or a technician. This person went home at night, laughed and played with his children, went to church on Sunday, and kissed his wife goodbye each morning.

Albert Speer did not personally design a death chamber, nor did he personally kill another human being but Albert Speer *did* use his brilliant technical expertise and talents to enable the most vicious and evil regime in history to murder untold millions of human beings. But, before we condemn him, as engineers and technicians, we should ask, is Speer so different from us? How many of us would be willing to almost sell our souls for the opportunity to work on an architectural project that had historic implications? How many of us are seemingly hardwired to solve a technical problem without even appreciating where that solution might lead? How many of us are almost unconscious of our innate ability to compartmentalize our emotions and our values? How many of us look at the world around us in purely practical and pragmatic terms, almost as if we are viewing life *through the eyes of a dead man*?

To many engineers, Speer and his experiences during the Second World War may seem irrelevant to our modern world. True, there is little chance (hopefully) of a highly industrialized western power waging a war of world conquest, yet the essential questions of value that Albert Speer faced can be found in the lives of many engineers and technical people. The technology that each of us has nurtured and developed may have transformed our landscape, but the moral issues we face are the same. You may be an engineer sitting in front of a CAD/CAM screen designing a seemingly benign component that will become part of some sophisticated weapons system that will be sold to unknown people in a far off land; you may design automobile parts and must make a value judgment between saving your company costs versus saving your customers' lives; or, perhaps, you're an engineer who worries that the miraculous pharmaceutical you helped your company develop may have long-term side effects that could cause cancer. In reality, almost every engineer in the course of their career faces some sort of moral issues.

In the following pages, the reader should observe Speer's personality and nuances and note how they match Florman's description of the technical personality. Place yourself, as an engineer, in Speer's shoes and honestly ask yourself, without the benefit of historical hindsight, "What would I have done?"

You will win early fame and retire early.[11]
—Speer's visit to a fortuneteller as a young man.

Albert Speer was born in the spring of 1905 in Mannheim, Germany to an upper middle-class family that had benefited from Germany's meteoric economic growth. Speer's maternal grandfather, the son of a poor forester from the Black Forest, took advantage of the opportunities of Germany's late-arriving industrial revolution to become one of the largest machine tool manufacturers in Germany. Speer's paternal grandfather also possessed a technical proficiency and became a well-known architect. Speer's father continued the family's technical tradition by also becoming an architect and establishing one of the more prosperous architecture firms in the area.

---

[11] A. Speer. 1970. *Inside the Third Reich* (The Macmillan Co.), p. 11.

In the years before the First World War, Albert Speer was provided a very comfortable childhood in a Germany that was expanding economically at a rate that made it the envy of the world. Growing up in this world, the young Albert Speer was a bit more frail than his brothers and schoolmates and was subject to occasional fainting spells. He also tended to be more serious and studious than his playmates and took an early interest and love for mathematics.

The First World War broke out in August 1914. The early years of the war brought occasional aerial bombings to Mannheim due to its proximity to the French border. These bombings, along with the massive destruction throughout most of Europe, were terrifying at the time; nevertheless, they were nothing compared to the merciless destruction that Speer was going to help unleash during the next war. Although the later years of the First World War brought significant hardships to most Germans, the Speers were able to endure these difficult times significantly better than other Germans.

Despite Woodrow Wilson's guarantee of a just and lasting European peace after such a savage war, the Treaty of Versailles did little but aggravate and eventually inflame the de-stabilizing trends that permeated Germany for most of its history. Since its unification in 1871, Germany, under the Kaisers, had nurtured strong feelings of nationalism bordering on paranoia. Situated in the middle of Europe between Russia and France, the Germans feared they were continually being encircled and were being denied their rightful place on the world stage. From its Prussian beginnings, the new German state relied heavily on the influence of the military in its culture and public life. In all other western countries of the time, the military was subservient to the state, but in Germany, it became the foundation of the state. These factors nurtured a German disposition demanding order and unquestioning loyalty to an absolutist state.

Speer recalled his school years during the post-war Weimar Republic where, despite the revolution and the installation of a democratic government, German society still had difficulty adjusting to western-style personal freedom and liberty. Politics was not to be discussed at school and, "… the traditional authorities were part of the God-given order of things."[12]

---

[12] A. Speer. n.d.. *Inside the Third Reich*, p. 8.

Students were told what to do and told what to think. They were raised in a society and a culture where they knew no other way. Even at home, in a time when most of Germany was in political and economic turmoil, politics was seldom discussed. Speer's father was a liberal who supported Germany's republican experiment, yet Speer maintained a total disinterest in politics. As he stated later in his autobiography:

> Father would have surely been glad to talk about politics with me, but I tended to dodge such discussions and he did not persist. The political indifference was characteristic of the youth of that period, tired and disillusioned as they were by a lost war, revolution, and inflation; but it prevented me from forming political standards, from setting up categories on which political judgments could be based.[13]

Interestingly, Speer makes little mention in his autobiography of any religious or spiritual influences other than the fact his family was Protestant and, as a young man, he formed a pantheistic *closeness with nature*[14] that allowed him a sense of solitude while, "… escaping the demands of a world grown increasingly complicated."[15] Later, while serving his sentence at Spandau Prison, he wrote his daughter, "My parents didn't go to church … and in the school the chaplain had the unintelligent habit of imposing learning of Psalms by heart as a punishment! …Your mother and I did marry in a church, but I can't claim to have felt anything then: we just did it to please her parents." And later in his letter to his daughter, he states: "When your mother and I did leave the [Protestant] church, it was in reaction to the political opposition of the churches to Hitler—I suppose it was a sort of statement of loyalty."[16]

Despite his upper-middle class lifestyle and his family's ability to survive both the Great War and the post-war tragedy of a defeated Germany, Albert Speer did not grow up in a warm or emotional household.

[13] Ibid. p 8.
[14] Ibid. p. 10.
[15] Ibid. p. 10.
[16] G. Sereny. n.d. *Albert Speer, His Battle With Truth*, p. 631.

He describes his grandmother as "… a serious woman, moored fast to simple notions about life and possessing an obstinate energy. She dominated everyone around her." She "… inspired in me more respect than love in my boyhood."[17] Speer's own mother had been described as *haughty* and *aloof.* Speer admired his father but found him distant and reserved. The German historian, Joachim Fest, described Speer's outlook toward his parents as *virtual strangers*[18] and described Albert as possessing a, "…lack of emotion and a shyness that was apparent at an early age."[19]

Later, in his twilight years, after completing his 20-year sentence for war crimes, Speer made friends with Father Athanasius, a Benedictine monk who said, "… everything about Speer was discipline. I often wondered what happened to him as a child to make him into what he was, a brilliant man incapable of abstract thinking and, I think, incapable of sensual love and thus, finally, an incomplete man." Speer, the architect, designed a chair for Father Athanasius once and told him it was a design he *loved.* Father Athanasius recalled, "It was the only time in the ten years I knew him that he pronounced the word, 'love.'"[20]

Speer graduated from high school in Weimar Germany, hoping to follow his natural inclination for mathematics and become a university professor. His father rejected the idea stating, "Can you imagine yourself spending your life in some backwater university? You'd never make any money. You'd probably end up cramming snotty-nosed little morons. Is that the life you want?"[21] Instead of debating or challenging the authority of his father, Albert Speer unquestioningly followed his father's advice and pursued the traditional family vocation of architecture.

In 1924, he went to the Institute of Technology in the city of Munich where Adolf Hitler was standing trial for high treason for his leadership and involvement in the previous year's *Beer Hall Putsch*, an ill-conceived and failed attempt to overthrow the Bavarian government. Although Hitler drew a sentence of five years, the authorities bent to public opinion

---

[17] A. Speer. n.d. *Inside the Third Reich*, p. 4.

[18] J. Fest. 1999. *Speer, The Final Verdict* (Harcourt Books), p. 14.

[19] Ibid. p. 11.

[20] G. Sereny n.d. *Albert Speer, His Battle With Truth*, p. 697.

[21] G. Sereny. n.d. *Albert Speer, His Battle With Truth*, p. 63.

when they released and pardoned him after serving just a few months—enough time to compose his book, *Mein Kampf*. Hitler attracted growing numbers of disillusioned and angry youths to his speeches and rallies in those years, yet Speer wrote, "I took little notice of him... I was studying far into the night."[22]

Later, after graduating, Speer became one of the youngest assistant professors at the age of 25. He was persuaded by his fellow students to attend a speech that Hitler was giving in a nearby beer hall. Speer, like many Germans, was swept away after his first encounter with the man who would soon change his life and nearly destroy western civilization. After the speech, he felt he had to be alone to think about what he just heard and to dissect the emotions he was feeling. That evening, Speer went for a long, solitary walk. The next morning, he joined the Nazi Party.

Much later, in his autobiography, Speer tried to comprehend the magnitude of what he did at such a young age. He could not understand how someone like him, a technical person, someone who relied solely on facts, could make such a monumental decision without fully understanding what he was committing to when he joined the Nazis. "As an intellectual I might have been expected to collect documentation with the same thoroughness and to examine various points of view with the same lack of bias that I learned to apply in my preliminary architectural studies. This failure was rooted in my inadequate political schooling. As a result, I remained uncritical, unable to deal with the arguments of my student friends, who were predominately indoctrinated with the National Socialist ideology." Twenty years later, while reflecting upon his life from a prison cell, with the hindsight of his ruined life and a ruined continent he continued, "Not to have worked that out for myself; not, given my education, to have read books, magazines, and newspapers of various viewpoints, not to have tried to see through the whole apparatus of mystification—was already criminal."[23]

Despite joining the party, Speer claims he was never an anti-Semite and even makes the claim, decades later, that he could hardly recall any

---

[22] A. Speer. n.d. *Inside the Third Reich*, p. 10.
[23] A. Speer. n.d. *Inside the Third Reich*, p. 19.

anti-Semite remarks made by Hitler.[24] Speer states that, "Political events did not concern me. I felt there was no need for me to take any political positions at all. …I was expected to confine myself to the job of building."[25] Truly a terrifying admission when one realizes Speer is referring to the destruction of the Jewish race simply and coldly as *political events* and *political positions*. It is just as unnerving to contemplate that a man with access to Hitler's inner circle, a man who attended most of Hitler's major speeches could state that he could hardly remember Hitler making anti-Semitic remarks because he was so intensely involved and focused on his technical work.

Perhaps even more telling of Speer's personality was his reaction to seeing the shattered Jewish storefronts and the smoldering fires from synagogues across Germany after *Kristallnacht*[26] when he confessed that, "… what really disturbed me at the time was the aspect of disorder that I saw on Fasanenstrasse: charred beams, collapsed facades, burned out

---

[24] Speer's attitude toward Jews and his responsibility for the Holocaust has been very well documented and debated and has been the subject of numerous historical studies. The most current thinking is that Speer was lying at the Nuremberg trials when he claimed he knew nothing of the mass murders. Most scholars now believe he may have presented a most clever and cunning defense by stating he wished to accept responsibility for the crimes of the Nazis on the basis that, as a technocrat, he helped the regime survive and prosper, yet he still knew nothing of the death camps. It has been acknowledged by most historians that Speer was at Himmler's terrifying speech in Posen in 1943 where Himmler made certain that all present understood that they were all just as responsible as he was for the mass murder of the Jews. This was the first time the Nazi hierarchy openly described the extermination that had been ongoing throughout eastern Europe. Himmler, in his disturbing logic, stated his sympathy with those who had to endure the crude and heartless work of killing women and children but assured them that future generations of Germans would be grateful. For further information, the reader should see, *Albert Speer, His Battle with Truth* by Gitta Sereny, *Speer, the Final Verdict* by Joachim Fest, or *Hitler's Engineers* by Blaine Taylor.

[25] A. Speer. n.d. *Inside the Third Reich*, p. 112.

[26] Kristallnacht, or the *Night of Broken Glass*, occurred on November 10–11, 1938, as a response to a German diplomat being assassinated in Paris by a young Jew. Hitler allowed his SA Stormtroopers to ravage Jewish homes, storefronts, and synagogues throughout Germany and Austria. By the time it was over, 91 Jews were killed and 30,000 Jewish men (nearly a quarter of all Jewish men living in Germany) were sent to concentration camps.

walls… The smashed window panes of shop windows offended my sense of middle-class order."[27]

Hitler's Architect

For the commission to do a great building, I would have sold my soul like Faust. Now I had found my Mephistopheles. He seemed no less engaging than Goethe's.

—Albert Speer[28]

In January of 1933, Hitler was appointed the German Chancellor. He spent the next 18 months cleverly and brutally consolidating his power until August of 1934 when he was proclaimed Fuhrer and held absolute power.

Speer's road to fame began soon after he joined the Nazi Party. By luck, he gained small architectural commissions from the party and soon became noticed for his efficiency and ability to meet tight schedules. These commissions grew in size, and Speer soon found himself working with Hitler himself in designing Hitler's vision of a future capital, Germania, intended to be representative of a triumphal Reich that would dominate the world.

Speer was just a young man who suddenly found himself to be the personal favorite of the most powerful man in Germany, a man worshiped by millions and feared by millions more. Hitler always considered himself an artist first, who only became a politician to make his dream of a powerful Germany realized. Hitler saw the young Speer as his unfulfilled self, as someone who was technically capable of achieving his artistic dreams for a future Germany that would rule the world.

The young architect was given the commission of planning the Nazi Party rallies held annually in Nuremberg and soon was given the commission that sealed his prominence as Hitler's favorite architect—the new Reich Chancellery. Speer managed to design and construct this formidable building within a year, much impressing Hitler with his incredible organizational skills.

---

[27] A. Speer. n.d. *Inside the Third Reich*, p. 111.

[28] Ibid. p. 31.

Speer was given increasing responsibility for designing buildings on a scale that was unsurpassed in history. When Speer designed the Nuremberg stadium, used for the annual Nazi rally, he constructed it with a term he coined as *ruin value*, meaning the buildings he designed would be built in such a fashion that they would last for thousands of years like the ancient ruins of Greece. This type of design concept matched perfectly with Hitler's concept of a *Thousand Year Reich* and Speer quickly moved into the Fuhrer's inner circle where Hitler shared his innermost dreams with his young architect.

For the Nazi Party rallies in Nuremberg, Speer created his famous *Cathedral of Light*. Speer commandeered almost every searchlight from throughout Germany and arranged them on the outside borders of the enormous, outdoor, nighttime rally. This gave a solemn, almost spiritual effect, as the searchlights shone toward the overhanging clouds. Foreign observers of the rally were stunned, not so much by Speer's artistry but by the apparent fact that Germany must have re-armed their military to such an extent that untold numbers of searchlights could be placed at a single rally.

Hitler wanted to make Berlin the future capital of his empire and he demanded that it be the most impressive city in the world. Hitler's capital was to be named *Germania*, and every visitor to it would feel overwhelmed by Germany's strength, power, and beauty. In Hitler's dream city of Germania, Speer had planned as the centerpiece a gargantuan domed *Great Hall* that would hold 180,000 occupants as they listened to the Fuhrer's speeches. Had it ever been built Speer's dome would have dwarfed any structure near it. Its volume could have contained several domes the size of the U.S. Capitol. Along the sprawling grand avenue leading to the Great Hall would be a German version of Paris' *Arc de Triumph*, but Hitler's arch would dwarf Napoleon's by being almost 2.5 times as tall. This was art and architecture based on ostentation and megalomania. Rather than show the might and power of a new Reich, Speer's plans for Germania revealed an inferiority complex that exemplified Nazi amateurishness and paranoia.[29]

---

[29] The Great Dome was so large, in fact, that the acoustics would have made it impossible for any of the 180,000 occupants to be able to hear anyone at the podium speaking. The city of Berlin, which was to be transformed into Hitler's

Figure 4.7 Hitler's dream, and Speer's design, for a new capital,
Germainia

Source: Commons: Bundesarchiv.

Albert Speer grew close to Hitler and soon had the single most favored spot within Hitler's circle. Hitler admired Speer's grandiose style of architecture, and he also formed a deep admiration for Speer. "In looks and language the tall, handsome young Speer probably came close to being a German ideal for the Austrian Hitler..."[30] For Adolf Hitler, idolized and worshiped by millions of Germans, Albert Speer came the closest to being a friend.

Germania, was built on converted swampland, and there are serious doubts that the ground would have been able to support the huge weight of such a structure. Speer, himself, during his imprisonment at Spandau worried that the condensation caused by 180,000 occupants within a closed dome may have caused vapor clouds to form within the structure, which could cause rain droplets to fall from clouds forming within the huge expanse of the dome.

[30] G. Sereny. n.d. *Albert Speer, His Battle With Truth*, p. 138.

Figure 4.8 Speer and his patron
Source: Commons: Bundesarchiv.

Speer, like many technical people, hated public speaking. Too often, those from the technical professions have an inability to relate to the human element during public speaking. Plus, they are notorious for their poor communication skills, having devoted most of their education to studying math and physics rather than language skills. On one occasion, Speer agreed to design a picture gallery in Hitler's hometown of Linz, Austria, only on the condition he would not be required to make a speech. Later on, public speaking became unavoidable for the architect who was becoming very well known. When the initial *East-West Axis* of Speer's new avenue through Berlin was completed, Speer could no longer avoid his fear of public speaking and was scheduled to speak before hundreds of invitees, including most of the Nazi hierarchy. Speer gave a two-sentence speech: "Mein Fuehrer, I herewith report the completion of the East-West Axis. May the work speak for itself!" Hitler, one of history's most persuasive orators used this event for years to tease Speer about his reluctance to engage an audience.[31]

---

[31] A. Speer. n.d. *Inside the Third Reich*, p. 148.

The young Speer felt the intoxication of power and, before long, would have to come to terms with his addiction to both his profession and to his patron who would soon bring him closer into the darkness being unleashed on the world.

I remember when Hitler gave me the assignment to build the Atlantic Wall, a system of fortifications from the North Cape to the Pyrenees, what feelings of exultation filled me when my signature could mean the expenditure of billions of marks and direct hundreds of thousands to construction sites. Only in retrospect do I become aware that as an architect at Hitler's side I was also seeking the pleasures of power.[32]

Minister of Armaments

I grow dizzy when I recall that the number of manufactured tanks seems to have been more important to me than the vanished victims of racism.

—Albert Speer[33]

In February of 1942, the German Army was stalled on the outskirts of Moscow because of the Russian winter. Since June of the previous year, Hitler's armies had moved relentlessly east, destroying everything in their path and capturing millions of Soviet soldiers who were either shipped westward for slave labor or simply left to die from exposure or starvation. Behind the German onslaught were the ghoulish *Einsatzgruppen*, SS killing squads who relentlessly searched village after village, beginning the systematic murder of the Jews throughout Eastern Europe.

Germany had conquered all of Europe and just as it seemed on the brink of crushing its most hated enemy, Soviet Russia, the German Minister of Armaments and Munitions, Dr. Fritz Todt, was killed in an airplane crash as he left *Wehrwolf*, Hitler's Eastern Front Headquarters located deep within the Ukraine. Before the war, Todt was known as the engineer

---

[32] A. Speer. 1976. *Spandau Diaries* (Macmillan), p. 406.
[33] A. Speer. n.d. *The Slave State*, Chapter 21.

who designed and built the German autobahn and became the regime's specialist for technical issues and problems. Once Hitler unleashed his forces against Europe, Todt, who was considered irreplaceable,[34] was in charge of supplying Hitler's armies with the munitions and weapons needed to conquer an empire stretching from North Africa to the Arctic and from France to Soviet Russia.

Speer happened to be at *Wehrwolf* as Todt left on his final voyage. Within a day of Todt's death, Hitler, in a surprising move, appointed his young, totally inexperienced architect to replace Todt as Minister of Armaments. Speer claims he was stunned so much that he requested Hitler formally command him to take on this new role for which he had no training or experience.[35] Decades later, some historians discounted Speer's description of shock at his appointment and claimed Speer was a young, ambitious technocrat who saw Germany on the brink of conquering the world and maneuvered himself into Hitler's inner circle just for such an opportunity. Regardless, Hitler recognized Speer's ability for organization and efficiency—traits common in almost every technical person.

The day before his appointment, Speer found himself lost while traveling through the frozen Ukrainian countryside where he encountered Russian peasants who helped treat his near frostbite condition. They helped him as a human being who was suffering, not as a despised conqueror who was destroying their country. Speer stated that, at the time, he felt *touched* by their kindness but simply could not understand it. Years later, while serving his sentence for crimes against humanity, he would begin to finally understand why these Russian peasants acted to help him.[36]

The German economy under Hitler's National Socialist regime was highly centralized and controlled and, as Reich Minister for Armaments, Speer commanded a massive sector of the German economy. Speer's genius was being able to organize and prioritize, and he had the ability to focus on what the German war machine's needs were and how to meet those needs. Speer understood how to use Hitler's backing to bulldoze

---

[34] A. Speer. n.d. *Inside the Third Reich*, p. 195.

[35] Ibid.

[36] Ibid. p. 524.

through the elaborate and inefficient Nazi bureaucracy and circumnavigate the corrupt and envious Nazi hierarchy.

Speer also had to guide an economy that was surprisingly not yet a full-fledged war economy as were the British, Russian, and American economies. Despite being an autocrat answerable to no one, Hitler constantly worried about German public opinion. He understood the fragility of power and knew that, despite his enormous political power, he could be toppled, should widespread discontent develop. To keep the German people distracted and content, Hitler refused to allow the war effort to interfere with the production of everyday consumer goods. But this all changed after the battle of Stalingrad in January of 1943. After this disastrous and pivotal loss, the German economy became totally devoted to the war effort.[37]

Because of the tremendous allied bombing campaign targeting German industrial centers, Speer instituted a policy of *Organized Improvisation*. Despite American and British bombers obliterating the huge factories feeding the Wehrmacht, Speer was actually able to increase German war production. Incredibly, amidst the widespread destruction on the home front, German production actually peaked as late as 1944. From a technical standpoint, this was an astonishing achievement. The American and British bombers devastated whole cities and entire industrial complexes, yet Speer was able to increase production by moving critical munitions work underground, rapidly repairing damaged factories, de-centralizing massive complexes, and scattering the production over a vast area, thus making it more difficult for allied bombers to locate and destroy.

---

[37] On February 18, 1943, at the Berlin Sportpalast, Hitler's propaganda chief, Josef Goebbels, gave his most famous speech sharing with the German people the monumental defeat at Stalingrad and bracing them for total war. "A merciless war is raging in the East. The Fuehrer was right when he said that in the end there will not be winners and losers, but the living and the dead. …We can no longer make only partial and careless use of the war potential at home and in the significant parts of Europe that we control. We must use our full resources, as quickly and thoroughly as it is organizationally and practically possible." Building his speech to its final crescendo, Goebbels screamed to a feverish and crazed audience: "I ask you: Do you want total war? If necessary, do you want a war more total and radical than anything that we can even imagine today?"

But hand-in-hand with Speer's genius for organization and his unwavering ability to accomplish almost impossible goals lie the methods he used to accomplish these goals. With millions of young German men serving on two fronts, there was a huge labor shortage in German industry. Unlike in Britain and America where women largely stepped in to fill these labor shortages, the Nazi ideology frowned on women working in factories. Speer needed men, and he consciously and intentionally turned to forcibly importing men from conquered countries to feed the German war economy. When that didn't fulfill his needs, he turned to slave labor—both captured prisoners of war and concentration camp labor. Speer now directed an enormous workforce of 28 million workers, of whom six million were forcibly imported into Germany from conquered countries and 60,000 were concentration camp prisoners.[38]

Speer was desperate to meet the munitions and armament requirements of the German armed forces in their titanic struggle to stop the Red Army's advance on the eastern front, the incessant bombings of German cities and industrial complexes by the British and American air forces, and the allied invasions of Italy and France. Speer knowingly and unhesitatingly requisitioned slave labor in order to solve the problems he confronted.

After visiting one of his steel plants where Russian prisoners of war were working as slave labor, Speer noticed the fear and terror in their eyes when he tried to inquire about their conditions. He wrote,

> But I asked no further questions. Why should I have done so; their expressions told me everything. If I were to try today to probe the feelings that stirred me then, if across the span of a lifetime I attempt to analyze what I really felt—pity, irritation, embarrassment, or indignation—it seems to me that the desperate race with time, my obsessional fixation on production and output statistics, blurred all considerations and feelings for humanity. An American historian has said of me that I loved machines more than people. He is not wrong. I realize that the sight of suffering

---

[38] G. Sereny. 2001. *The Healing Wound: Experiences and Reflections, Germany, 1938-2001* (Norton & Co.), p. 280.

people influenced only my emotions, but not my conduct. ... I continued to be ruled by the principles of utility.[39]

Later, during cross-examination at Nuremberg by the American prosecutor, Chief Justice Robert H. Jackson, Speer stated for the court his totally pragmatic outlook toward slave labor: "It is clear that a worker who has not enough food cannot achieve a good work output. I already said yesterday that every head of a plant, and I too at the top, was naturally interested in having well-fed and satisfied workers, because badly fed, dissatisfied workers make more mistakes and produce poor results."[40] Rather than being ruled by a moral law, Speer found himself "ruled by the principles of utility."

Speer once visited the concentration camp at Mauthausen in Austria and was given the VIP tour, devised by the SS to limit exposure to anything disturbing. Speer stated that a colleague had visited the death camp at Auschwitz in Poland and warned him never to go there. But, still, "I did not query him, I did not query Himmler, I did not query Hitler, I did not speak with personal friends. I did not investigate—for I did not want to know what was happening there... From that moment on, I was inescapably contaminated morally; from fear of discovering something which might have made me turn from my course, I had closed my eyes."[41]

Because of his technical genius, Speer was able to give Hitler and his armies the armaments needed to prolong the most murderous and devastating of all wars for at least an additional year.[42]

Götterdämmerung

No city will be left in the enemy's hands unless it's a heap of ruins.[43]

—Adolf Hitler

---

[39] A. Speer. n.d. *Inside the Third Reich*, p. 375.

[40] Justice R.H. Jackson. n.d. *The Cross-Examination of Albert Speer*, www.law.umkc.edu/faculty/projects/ftrials/nuremberg/speer.html.

[41] A. Speer. n.d. *Inside the Third Reich*, p. 375.

[42] A. Speer. April 24, 1971. *Long, Long Days With the Fuehrer* (Life Magazine).

[43] A. Speer. n.d. *The Spandau Diaries*, p. 200.

By February 1943, after the disaster at Stalingrad, the German advance to the east had stopped and was now slowly retreating westward. That summer, after the enormous tank battle at Kursk where Hitler gambled and lost everything on one final, overwhelming battle, most of the German staff understood the war was lost and defeat was simply a matter of time. Not only were German troops retreating from the Red Army in the east, but American and British bombers were completely devastating German cities such as Berlin, Cologne, Hamburg, Frankfurt, Nuremburg and, of course, Dresden.[44] All but the most fanatical Nazi understood, after the allied landing on D-day, that the war was hopelessly lost.

In March of 1945, with the Red Army on the outskirts of the capital, Speer learned that Goebbels had intended to call up all the last reserves for the final battle of Berlin. These reserves included not only young children and old men but also the members of the Berlin Philharmonic Orchestra. Speer foiled Goebbels' plan and had the musicians' papers shredded. He saw no need for some of Germany's greatest artists to be sent to a certain and needless death. Speer arranged a concert to be held in April at the Berlin Philharmonic Hall. Amidst the dying days of the Thousand Year Reich, in an unheated, unlit hall the audience huddled in their overcoats and listened to Wagner's *Twilight of the Gods*. At the exits, knowing the end was very near, Hitler Youth were handing out potassium cyanide capsules to those Berliners who preferred a painless death rather than face the vengeful soldiers of the Red Army who were now at the gates.[45]

---

[44] In Richard Overy's, *Interrogations: The Nazi Elite in Allied Hands, 1945*, the author relates the effect of the Allied strategic bombing of German cities. Perhaps the most interesting detail, from a military standpoint, is the revelation from several of the prisoners (particularly Goering) of the effect of allied airpower to bring about the German collapse. Goering believed that a one-on-one fight with the Russians would have resulted in a clear and overwhelming German victory. Allied air superiority managed to confound the German armaments and the transportation and communication systems within the Reich. The German general, Alfred Jodl, stated that aerial bombing also had a tremendous effect on the common soldier fighting at the front who felt helpless and hopeless knowing that his family was endangered while he was fighting in far off Soviet Russia.

[45] According to Antony Beevor's account in *The Fall of Berlin*, the Red Army raped and pillaged East Prussia, Pomerania, and Silesia on their way to Stalin's

Speer was certainly intelligent enough to understand the war was lost and also realize the repercussions for Germany of losing history's most destructive war. Speer began to recognize that not only had Hitler brought Germany into a war of annihilation in which Germany was completely devastated, but Hitler was now proposing an even more radical phase of the war that would clearly wipe out the German nation.

Finally, Speer began to comprehend his own involvement in the war and his own personal culpability in the death of millions of human beings. "To this day I shudder at the thought of what that regime had led me to—I who had once wanted nothing more than to be Hitler's master builder… For years I had lived in his entourage where human life meant nothing; but all that seemed to be none of my affair. Now I realized that this atmosphere had not left me untouched. I was just as entangled in a thicket of deceptions, intrigues, baseness, and killing. I myself had become part of this perverted world. For twelve years I had lived thoughtlessly among murderers."[46]

Speer slowly grew apart from Hitler as the war was now being waged on German soil. For Speer, his moral epiphany came when Hitler ordered the *Nero Order*. Hitler was determined that if the German people could not accomplish his dreams of a world dominated by a master race, then they had no justification to live. Hitler wanted the conquering armies to be left with nothing but a desolate and ruined country. Hitler ordered Speer to destroy the infrastructure of the German economy before the allied armies could attain control of Germany.

---

prize of Berlin. This brutality happening to German civilians in the path of the Soviet Army was publicized and broadcast throughout Germany by Goebbels in hopes it would rally German citizens to fight to the death out of fear of facing Soviet soldiers. Women paid a particularly horrible price for the savage devastation the Wehrmacht and SS caused in their attempt to conquer Russia. Once the Soviet troops took Berlin, an estimated 100,000 women were raped, and perhaps as many 10,000 women committed suicide to escape being raped. Overall, the Soviet Army raped two million German women by war's end. According to Catherine Merridale in her book, *Ivan's War*, Stalin encouraged his troops to impregnate as many women as possible in order to spread Soviet blood westward into Europe.

[46] A. Speer. n.d. *Inside the Third Reich*, p. 430.

Figure 4.9 A dejected and exhausted Speer shortly before the end
Source: Commons: Bundesarchiv.

Speer understood that to do so would mean the continuation of the suffering and death of the German people even after the war. By destroying the electrical grid, the water systems, the bridges, and the means of production life would become nearly impossible for the defeated German people. Speer, to his credit, made it his responsibility to counter Hitler's orders and sabotage his plan for a scorched earth.

Speer knew he was putting his life at risk to countermand Hitler. By the end of the war, Hitler was in a satanic rage against his generals and his staff and placed blame on all of them for the war's failure. Hitler trusted no one and had no remorse at killing anyone he considered a traitor.[47] Hitler had no respect for human life and even less for those who dared to interfere with his command. He ordered his army to shoot all

---

[47] This point is clearly seen when Berlin was encircled by the Red Army and everyone knew it would be simply a matter of days before the end; Hitler had Eva Braun's brother-in-law shot for treason when he tried to escape Berlin for safety. The next day Hitler married Eva Braun, and they both committed suicide.

deserters and traitors on sight. On the Eastern Front, he had over 10,000 of his own soldiers—nearly a division—shot for treason or cowardice. Often the bodies would be hung on the side of roads, with a sign warning other German soldiers of the price for treason. Despite the personal risk involved, Speer used the privileged powers of his office to travel around the country that was now being inundated by enemy troops in an attempt to prevent Hitler's *Nero Orders* from being carried out.

Speer, although feeling at times a hatred for Hitler, felt a personal obligation to return to Hitler's Berlin bunker one last time to say goodbye to the man who had changed his life. Descending the stairs 50 ft. under a bombed-out Berlin to a bunker made of tons of reinforced concrete, Hitler and Speer shared an emotional final meeting.

> During the last months I had hated him at times, fought him, lied to him, and deceived him, but at this moment I was confused and emotionally shaken. In this state I confessed to him that I had not carried out any demolitions but had actually prevented them. For a moment his eyes filled with tears.[48]

With the sounds of the Russian shelling reverberating through the walls of the bunker, Speer confessed to his former patron but also told the deranged dictator that he was still loyal to him. A bloodthirsty Hitler could not bring himself to kill the man who had shared his artist's dreams and had once built elaborate indoor models of the future Germania, the man who had organized German industry to feed his war machine, and the man who Hitler had once even considered to be his successor. Speer, shaken, left Hitler and walked out of the Fuhrerbunker into the burning streets of Berlin.

The Dangers of the Technocrat

Well, if you're such an expert, measure a man's soul; tell me how large or how small that is. You can define a straight line; what use is that to you if you've no idea what straightness means in life?

—Seneca, Letters from a Stoic

---

[48] A. Speer. n.d. *Inside the Third Reich*, p. 480.

Albert Speer was soon captured by British forces and, along with the remaining Nazi elite, was tried at Nuremberg, the city once famous for Hitler's rallies and Speer's *Cathedral of Light*. Despite his lawyer's advice, Speer was the only defendant who admitted guilt. Speer devised a complicated defense stating, on the one hand, that as a high official in the Reich government, he must be held accountable for its actions but, on the other hand, that he was not personally involved in the more horrid crimes committed by Hitler and his henchmen.

> My responsibility for the deportation of foreign workers was stated; then that I had opposed Himmler's plans solely on tactical grounds of their effect on production but had used concentration camp inmates without protest and had requisitioned Soviet prisoners of war for work in the armaments industry. It added to my culpability that I had raised no humane or ethical considerations in these cases, thus helping to forge the policy of raising foreign laborers by force.[49]

Speer claimed that he was simply a technical person, an architect, and was unaware of the crimes being committed by the Nazi regime until it was almost too late. Speer asserted that his real crime was ambition, and he did what almost any other architect would have done in his place. Speer was able to distance himself from the other, crude and unrepentant Nazis standing trial with him and also displayed a contrasting personal charm permitting him to be known as the *good Nazi* in the western press. The court favorably viewed Speer's initiative to prevent Hitler's scorched-earth policy and sentenced him to 20 years imprisonment.[50]

Speer, as all the Nazi defendants, was continually interviewed and analyzed by a variety of allied doctors, lawyers, and intellectuals. Speer was different from all the rest: "Whereas most of his fellow prisoners

---

[49] A. Speer. n.d. *Inside the Third Reich*, p. 522.

[50] Speer's defense at his trial has been controversial. Many historians now believe 20 years was much too lenient despite his willingness to accept responsibility. Since his death in 1981, more evidence has been uncovered, suggesting he was not the *good Nazi*, but the *clever Nazi*.

were unmitigated thugs, Speer, by contrast, is a charming, cultivated and intelligent man. It was these qualities combined with a conscience that subordinated everything to ambition, that made him one of the most dangerous of all Nazis."[51]

Speer exemplifies what happens when a technical person becomes too absorbed in his work. Speer understood this, not only in how it applied to himself but also in how he could utilize this personality defect in those who worked for him:

> Basically I exploited the phenomenon of the technician's often blind devotion to his task. Because of what seems to be the moral neutrality of technology, these people were without any scruples about their activities. The more technical the world imposed on us by the war, the more dangerous was this indifference of the technician to the direct consequences of his anonymous behavior.[52]

Speer was one of the most dangerous men in the 20th century, not because he personally killed anyone, but because he permitted his incredible skills to be manipulated and used by the most evil man in history. Speer, although extremely intelligent, willfully closed his eyes and helped perpetuate the vulgarity and death that was all around him. It was almost too late in his life, and certainly too late for western civilization, when Speer finally realized his horrific personal failures.

When he was still young enough to change course, before he was completely enveloped in the perverted and gruesome Nazi world, he witnessed *Kristallnacht*, the *Night of the Broken Glass*, when Hitler ordered his henchmen to burn Jewish synagogues and smash Jewish storefronts. Speer was unable to have the human feelings of revulsion and disgust and, instead, could only feel like an engineer and become uncomfortable by the disorder he saw in the streets of Berlin.

Speer saw his work as goal-oriented, and if he were in danger of missing his "desperate race with time" or his "obsessional fixation on

---

[51] J.K. Galbraith and G. W. Ball. December 17, 1945. *The Interrogation of Albert Speer* (LIFE Magazine)

[52] A. Speer. n.d. *Inside the Third Reich*, p. 212.

production," he was willing to make the moral decision to tear families apart and forcibly import foreign labor. When that didn't satisfy the beast, he was feeding he resorted to "burying his head" and using slave labor and then, the most helpless of all, the concentration camp inmates.

Speer spent the 20 years of his captivity trying to come to terms with himself, trying to understand how he allowed himself to become subservient to the most immoral and demonic regime in history. He realized that for most of his life, burying himself in his work was "… an unconscious effort to anesthetize his conscience."[53] He foresaw the future, the future that we now live in, as dependent upon the wonders created by the engineer and technician and that, "… the more technological the world becomes, the more essential will be the demand for individual freedom and the self-awareness of the individual human being as a counterpoise to technology."[54]

As we saw earlier, Florman described the typical characteristics of the engineering personality as: cautious, hardworking, dependable, orderly, pragmatic, and overly serious. Now, after reviewing Speer's life, we can see how these seemingly respectable traits of a good engineer can be twisted and exploited and, in the process, become the engineer's most vulnerable and dangerous attributes.

Speer's life represents an extreme case of an individual possessing these characteristics who was devoid of any ethical and moral values and was consumed by his technical profession that allowed him to view the world *through the eyes of a dead man*. Speer valued expediency and efficiency over the human values of dignity and justice. But, in reviewing his life, how far off was Speer's claim at his trial that he was simply doing what most any other architect would have done? How many times are we struck with the similarities to our own? He was "…too busy studying far into the night…" to even discuss the political world exploding all around him and because he was lacking in the ability to think discriminatively and critically, he found himself, "unable to deal with the arguments" of his friends.

Hitler and his henchmen inspired the evil that culminated in the Holocaust. But they were not alone; there were millions that also contributed

---

[53] G. Sereny. n.d. *Albert Speer, His Battle With Truth*, p. 222.
[54] A. Speer. n.d. *Inside the Third Reich*, p. 521.

either directly by actively participating or indirectly by their silence and disregard. And there were also engineers, technicians, and architects whose amoral technical ability and organizational genius proved essential in supporting an evil that almost destroyed our western civilization.

A man who once controlled the productive output of a modern industrial empire found himself alone in a bleak, cold, gray prison cell thinking of his past and what went wrong. Speer was guarded by Soviet soldiers whom he knew must have suffered tremendously during the war. Twenty million Russians were killed in four years by the German army that Speer fed with bullets, tanks, and bombs. On the Eastern Front, 20 Soviet soldiers had died for every German soldier killed.[55] The German war machine killed soldiers and civilians mercilessly and indiscriminately; essentially every Russian family felt the pain of a lost family member. Yet, none of these Russian prison guards at Spandau Prison in Berlin showed Speer any enmity, rather, he "... encountered uncorrupted feelings of sympathy, helpfulness, human understanding, feelings that bypassed the

Figure 4.10 A row of lampposts along the Strasse des 17 Juni in Berlin are the only surviving architectural works of Albert Speer within the city of Berlin

Source: Wikipedia.

---

[55] C. Merridale. n.d. *Ivan's War.*

prison rules."[56] He then recalled his meeting, long ago, with the Ukrainian peasants who saved him from frostbite. Speer finally understood what he couldn't comprehend back then—the value of genuine human kindness. "I forgot that humanity is the most important part of life."[57]

Questions to Consider

- At the Nuremberg Tribunal, the Allies believed, at least some of Speer's remorse, and sentenced him to 20 years imprisonment. Do you think justice was served?
- As we saw with Herbert Hoover, engineers have some difficulty adapting to politics. Speer stated that he simply chose to ignore the demonic politics happening around him and focused only on his job. Do you believe him? If true, does this exonerate Speer from guilt?
- After Speer's death, historians have greatly revised their view of him. Now, most believe Speer was lying, and that he absolutely knew of the death camps and had even demanded slave labor for his armament programs. Historians now believe he was so intellectually commanding that he was able to contrive the perfect defense to avoid hanging at Nuremberg. If he is now considered a criminal Nazi, should his book, *Inside the Third Reich* continue to be sold?
- As the Second World War was ending, the Cold War with the Soviet Union was beginning. The American government began *Operation Paperclip* to gather the many brilliant German engineers and scientists, such as Werner von Braun, and bring them back to the United States to help American technological progress and, also, to keep the Soviets from capturing them. Many of these Germans were seriously compromised, like Speer, but started a fresh, new beginning in the United States without any worry of being tried for war crimes. Was this wrong?

---

[56] Ibid. p. 524.
[57] BBC. n.d. *Visions of Space: Size Matters, Albert Speer*, Part 7 of 7.

Afterword

In 1867, after the Industrial Revolution had changed the very fabric of English life, the philosopher and champion of individual liberty, John Stuart Mill, delivered his inaugural address as Lord Rector of the University of St. Andrews. He broached *the great controversy* of the day: should a student be taught the classics—literature, languages and philosophy—or should he be taught the practical sciences that drive industry? Mill answered, "This question, whether we should be taught the classics or the sciences, seems to me, I confess, very like a dispute whether painters should cultivate drawing or coloring, or … whether a tailor should make coats or trousers. I can only reply by the question, why not both?"

> Can anything deserve the name of a good education which does not include literature and science too? If there were no more to be said than that scientific education teaches us to think, and literary education to express our thoughts, do we not require both? and is not any one a poor, maimed, lopsided fragment of humanity who is deficient in either?[1]

A century and a half after Mill's address, during our Fifth Year Forum at the Astronaut Beach House, we were still trying to answer that question. One of our attendees remarked that their school had, indeed, once recognized that four years simply weren't enough to fully educate an engineering student. To correct this, they went against the norm and made their bachelor's in engineering a five-year degree. The result? A drastic loss of students and applications as parents who were footing the bill for the already-high tuition costs didn't want a fifth year of tuition bills. The free market won, and the experiment didn't last long.

Does this mean you're on your own if you wish to enhance your professional skills? Hardly. Most corporations and organizations I have dealt

---

[1] John Stuart Mill Inaugural Address University of St. Andrews. 1867.

with are anxious to see their technical employees gain additional training in communications, critical thinking, and ethics. Afterall, these additional skills make you a more valuable asset to their company. In most cases, it just takes the realization and the initiative on your part to acquire such training.

There are also countless avenues for personal training available on websites, online universities, virtual forums and lectures, and so on.

STEM fields and careers are a most noble way for an individual to make a living. As a professional, you have the opportunity, and the skills, to make the world a better place with the technologies you understand so well. Almost everything we rely on today to make our lives easier, more efficient, safer, healthier, and more satisfied is a result of STEM. What you do enhances the lives of everyone.

The purpose of this book is certainly not to degrade four very difficult and arduous years spent to earn an engineering or technical degree. On the contrary, those four years and the subjects mastered are essential to having an effective STEM career. Rather, the purpose of this book is to help you enhance your hard-earned education and the STEM skills you worked so hard to master.

Communication proficiency, an understanding of critical thinking skills, and appreciating the moral responsibility behind technical expertise and prowess shouldn't be known simply as *soft skills*. These abilities should be known as *professional skills* because these are the skills beyond differential equations, thermodynamics, electric circuits, mechanics of materials, and so on that will allow you to become not only a better engineer but also a better person.

About the Author

Mr. Forsgren started his career as a mechanic apprentice at NASA's Glenn Research Center in Cleveland, Ohio and, after 10 years of night school, earned an undergraduate and then graduate degree in engineering. In 2005, Mr. Forsgren transferred to NASA Headquarters in Washington D.C. to manage agency training efforts and in 2013 was appointed the director of the Academy of Program/Project and Engineering Leadership (APPEL). In 2016 he was given the additional responsibility of serving as the NASA Chief Knowledge Officer until his retirement in 2021. He is also the author of, *Lean Knowledge Management: How NASA Implemented a Practical KM Program.* Mr. Forsgren can be contacted at rforsgren4@gmail.com

Index

**OTHER TITLES IN THE PORTFOLIO AND
PROJECT MANAGEMENT COLLECTION**

Timothy J. Kloppenborg, Xavier University and
Kam Jugdev, Athabasca University, Editors

- *Project Control Methods and Best Practices* by Yakubu Olawale
- *Managing Projects With PMBOK 7* by James W. Marion and Tracey Richardson
- *Shields Up* by Gregory J. Skulmoski
- *Greatness in Construction History* by Sherif Hashem
- *The Inner Building Blocks* by Abhishek Rai
- *Project Profitability* by Reginald Tomas Lee
- *Moving the Needle With Lean OKRs* by Bart den Haak
- *Lean Knowledge Management* by Roger Forsgren
- *The MBA Distilled for Project & Program Professionals* by Bradley D. Clark
- *Project Management for Banks* by Dan Bonner
- *Successfully Achieving Strategy Through Effective Portfolio Management* by Frank R. Parth
- *Be Agile Do Agile* by Vittal Anantatmula and Timothy J. Kloppenborg

Concise and Applied Business Books

The Collection listed above is one of 30 business subject collections that Business Expert Press has grown to make BEP a premiere publisher of print and digital books. Our concise and applied books are for…

- Professionals and Practitioners
- Faculty who adopt our books for courses
- Librarians who know that BEP's Digital Libraries are a unique way to offer students ebooks to download, not restricted with any digital rights management
- Executive Training Course Leaders
- Business Seminar Organizers

Business Expert Press books are for anyone who needs to dig deeper on business ideas, goals, and solutions to everyday problems. Whether one print book, one ebook, or buying a digital library of 110 ebooks, we remain the affordable and smart way to be business smart. For more information, please visit www.businessexpertpress.com, or contact sales@businessexpertpress.com.

www.ingramcontent.com/pod-product-compliance
Lightning Source LLC
Chambersburg PA
CBHW061322220326
41599CB00026B/4991